NEW DIRECTIONS FOR INSTITUTIONAL RESEARCH

J. Fredericks Volkwein, *Penn State University*
EDITOR-IN-CHIEF

Larry H. Litten, *Dartmouth College*
ASSOCIATE EDITOR

Analyzing Costs in Higher Education: What Institutional Researchers Need to Know

Michael F. Middaugh
University of Delaware

EDITOR

Number 106, Summer 2000

JOSSEY-BASS PUBLISHERS
San Francisco

ANALYZING COSTS IN HIGHER EDUCATION:
WHAT INSTITUTIONAL RESEARCHERS NEED TO KNOW
Michael F. Middaugh (ed.)
New Directions for Institutional Research, no. 106
Volume XXVII, Number 2
J. Fredericks Volkwein, Editor-in-Chief

New Directions for Institutional Research is indexed in *College Student
Personnel Abstracts, Contents Pages in Education,* and *Current Index to Journals in Education* (ERIC).

Microfilm copies of issues and chapters are available in 16mm and 35mm,
as well as microfiche in 105mm, through University Microfilms Inc., 300
North Zeeb Road, Ann Arbor, Michigan 48106-1346.

ISSN 0271-0579   ISBN 0-7879-5437-3

NEW DIRECTIONS FOR INSTITUTIONAL RESEARCH is part of The Jossey-Bass
Higher and Adult Education Series and is published quarterly by Jossey-
Bass Inc., Publishers, 350 Sansome Street, San Francisco, California
94104-1342 (publication number USPS 098-830). Periodicals postage
paid at San Francisco, California, and at additional mailing offices. POST-
MASTER: Send address changes to New Directions for Institutional
Research, Jossey-Bass Inc., Publishers, 350 Sansome Street, San Francisco,
California 94104-1342.

SUBSCRIPTIONS cost $56.00 for individuals and $99.00 for institutions,
agencies, and libraries.

EDITORIAL CORRESPONDENCE should be sent to J. Fredericks Volkwein,
Center for the Study of Higher Education, Penn State University, 403
South Allen Street, Suite 104, University Park, PA 16801-5252.

Photograph of the library by Michael Graves at San Juan Capistrano by
Chad Slattery © 1984. All rights reserved.

www.josseybass.com

Printed in the United States of America on acid-free recycled paper containing 100 percent recovered waste paper, of which at least 20 percent is
postconsumer waste.

THE ASSOCIATION FOR INSTITUTIONAL RESEARCH was created in 1966 to bene-fit, assist, and advance research leading to improved understanding, planning, and operation of institutions of higher education. Publication policy is set by its Publications Committee.

For information about the Association for Institutional Research, write to the following address:

AIR Executive Office
114 Stone Building
Florida State University
Tallahassee, FL 32306-4462

(850) 644-4470

air@mailer.fsu.edu
http://airweb.org

CONTENTS

EDITOR'S NOTES

For the past several years, Fred Volkwein, editor-in-chief of *New Directions for Institutional Research* (NDIR), and I have had a running conversation about the need for a volume on cost studies and expenditure analysis. For a wide variety of reasons, not the least being pressure from parents, state legislatures, and Congress, institutional researchers have been asked to become increasingly involved in the world of financial data. Most of our colleagues in institutional research are not trained economists or accountants, and much of the terrain in financial analysis is therefore new to them. Consequently, Fred Volkwein and I thought that an NDIR volume that gave a broad overview of the issues and strategies entailed in conducting cost studies would be particularly useful.

I suspect that I was asked to edit this volume for a number of reasons. For the past decade, much of my professional life has been spent in directing a national data-sharing effort commonly referred to as the Delaware Study of Instructional Costs and Productivity. I have also been involved in the redesign activities for the IPEDS Finance Survey and have acted as an unpaid consultant to both the National Center for Education Statistics (NCES) and the National Association of College and University Business Officers (NACUBO) as they developed their national studies of the cost of higher education, both of which are under way at this writing. One might think that I have extensive financial background, based on the activities in which I am involved. I do not. I have numerous battle scars earned from trial-and-error experience in doing cost studies. More important, I am blessed with friends and colleagues who know far more than I do and who have shared their expertise with me over the years. Seven of those colleagues have contributed chapters to this book.

Paul T. Brinkman is associate vice president for budget and planning at the University of Utah and is no stranger to the economics of higher education. I first met Paul in the late 1980s when he was working for the National Center for Higher Education Management Systems, where he specialized in cost studies. When I assembled the first Delaware Study Advisory Committee in 1995, Paul agreed to serve and has continued to do so to date. He has been a key part of the success of that study. Paul opens this volume with an excellent overview of the major issues involved in the economics of higher education. This is a wonderful summary for those taking the first step in thinking about college cost.

Like Paul T. Brinkman, Frances L. Dyke, director of institutional research at the University of Oregon, has served on the Delaware Study Advisory Committee since its inception. I first met Frances in 1995 and was immediately impressed with her ability to embrace complex issues and reduce them to their component parts in ways that were straightforward and easy to understand. It is that gift and facility that make her chapter on

1

understanding expenditure data so remarkable. For the institutional researcher who has never tackled a financial balance sheet, this chapter is the perfect road map.

When I chaired the National Postsecondary Education Cooperative work group on redesign of the IPEDS Finance Survey, a central task was evaluating what needed to go into the congressionally mandated NCES national study of higher education costs. As we sifted through background material, one name kept surfacing. Gordon C. Winston, professor of economics at Williams College, has written extensively on the issue of developing a full-cost model for higher education. He has been particularly insistent that any such model must account for the capital assets of an institution. His work caught the attention of the National Commission on the Cost of Higher Education, which was created by Congress in 1998. When I called Gordon and asked him if he would be willing to write on the subject of full costing, he readily agreed. I think you will find his chapter to be particularly thought-provoking and useful.

The first three chapters of this volume are intended to provide a conceptual framework for thinking about cost studies. The remainder of the volume describes practical issues in executing such studies.

In Chapter Four, Kelli J. Armstrong, who in my view is one of the bright, emerging new talents in institutional research, describes issues and strategies surrounding the building of a consistent and reliable financial database on campus. She rightly notes that most institutional research offices lack the in-house expertise to create such a database, and she describes the necessary campus alliances that must be forged to ensure both accuracy and credibility of financial information as well as strategies for presenting it to nonfinancial campus types. Kelli brings to the chapter her work experience, which embraces a major private research university, a state higher education board, and the president's office of a major public system.

In Chapter Five, I draw on the data that Kelli J. Armstrong has developed in the previous chapter and describe strategies for making interinstitutional comparisons of data. Not surprisingly, the chapter includes a discussion of the Delaware Study of Instructional Costs and Productivity, which involves data sharing among hundreds of institutions in the areas of teaching loads, instructional costs, and research and service productivity at the academic-discipline level of analysis. The chapter also reviews a number of public domain data sources for academic and administrative information sharing.

I have always thought that the only point in collecting data is that it be used in decision making and policy development at the most senior levels of institutional management. Fortunately for me, I have enjoyed the enthusiastic encouragement and support of two key administrators at the University of Delaware, David E. Hollowell, executive vice president to whom I directly report, and Melvyn D. Schiavelli, provost and one of the most visionary academic leaders with whom one might hope to work. Many of my colleagues in institutional research frequently complain that they never know what the real informational needs of senior management are. That has not been a problem for me at the University of Delaware, where both Dave and Mel are very forthcoming about their academic and administrative data needs. When I asked them to put some general thoughts in that regard on paper, they responded enthusiastically with Chapter Six in this volume.

All of the talk about college costs has prompted not only institutional analyses of expenditures and cost drivers but national attempts as well. In Chapter Seven, Travis J. Reindl, policy analyst at the American Association of State Colleges and Universities, looks at two of the more prominent efforts—the congressionally mandated study of higher education costs being undertaken by NCES and a parallel effort sponsored by NACUBO.

All of the authors involved in this project have enjoyed the opportunity to develop their thoughts on collecting and using expenditure data. I believe that they have provided us with valuable insights and strategic direction, and I hope that you find this volume useful as you embark on conducting relevant cost studies.

Michael F. Middaugh
Editor

MICHAEL F. MIDDAUGH is assistant vice president for institutional research and planning at the University of Delaware.

1

Perspectives drawn from the economics of higher education reveal the many dimensions of higher education costs.

The Economics of Higher Education: Focus on Cost

Paul T. Brinkman

Perhaps at no time in our history has the subject of higher education costs had a higher profile than at present. From homes to state capitols to the halls of Congress, those costs have become an issue, even a contentious one at times as the work of The National Commission on the Cost of Higher Education (1998) clearly demonstrates.

For a long time, our national strategy was to find ways to help students meet the costs of attending college, whatever the magnitude of those costs might be. The GI Bill and Social Security programs that were major sources of funding for students in the 1950s and 1960s, the explosive growth of federal student aid in the 1970s and of state student aid in the 1980s, and federal tax credits in the 1990s all represent the enormous effort that has been made to help students afford higher education. Through their own student aid programs, colleges and universities have also played a major role in helping with the financial burden for some students.

Despite this very considerable effort, the perception in recent years has been that we are falling short of our goal. Accordingly, attention has shifted. We as a nation are still actively engaged in trying to find more money to support students and to find new ways to help families save for college expenses, but we are now looking intently at the other side of the equation as well, at costs incurred by colleges and universities, or *supplier costs*. The public is asking whether those costs are out of control and what the government's role has been and should be in this matter.

This is hardly a new pattern in our social and economic life. Arguably any significant component of our personal or collective budgets that grows faster than the average rate for other things we buy will eventually be

NEW DIRECTIONS FOR INSTITUTIONAL RESEARCH, no. 106, Summer 2000   © Jossey-Bass Publishers noticed and addressed. Health care comes immediately to mind, of course. We have made great efforts as a nation to cover buyer costs and continue to do so, but increasingly we have been focusing on supplier costs.

Efforts to control supplier costs are grounded on assumptions about the relationship between costs borne by suppliers and the prices they charge, a relationship that is exceptionally complex in higher education. It is too much to say that those costs and prices are independent of one another in higher education, but they are far from perfectly correlated. Therefore, the increased attention given to supplier costs may or may not affect supplier prices in higher education in the manner desired, but greater scrutiny should at least lead to greater understanding of those costs.

The next section of this chapter begins with an overview of several cost-related themes in the economics of higher education. Then the discussion turns to selected perspectives on supplier costs in higher education, the methods used to determine supplier costs, and the factors that influence those costs.

Economics of Higher Education: An Overview

It is difficult to know what to expect when reading a book or an article on the economics of higher education. For example, in a short article on the subject, Hawkins (1998) manages to discuss trust markets, the extent to which colleges are like or unlike businesses, tuition and other student expenses, supplier costs, student financial aid, the composition of the consumer price index (CPI), measures of median family income, wage differentials accorded college graduates, academic drift, and the need to develop better measures of higher education output. This diversity of issues notwithstanding, the cost-related topics that fall within the economics of higher education tend to cluster around four general themes: students as consumers, institutions as suppliers, higher education as a market, and higher education as a variety of investments. A brief section on each follows. The comments are meant in part as signposts for readers on unfamiliar terrain.

Consumers. Although higher education has an extensive array of consumers of its many products and services, economic analysis has been focused on students, particularly with respect to their sensitivity to prices, or *buyers' costs,* and to price discounts. Numerous studies have addressed these two topics. Heller (1997) and Paulsen (1998) provide recent summaries of findings on price elasticities and on the effects of student financial aid. Economists have also analyzed the overall effectiveness of programs designed to ensure access to higher education (for example, McPherson and Shapiro, 1997).

The many complexities aside, a brief summary of findings would be as follows. Students do respond to prices and price discounts. Low-income students and black students are especially responsive to both. Students may respond differently to different types of prices (tuition versus other costs of attendance). Not all types of financial aid are equally effective; for example, students tend to prefer grants to loans or work-study. Student financial aid works to enhance access and choice, other things being equal, but many other factors are involved in decisions related to attending college. The overall effectiveness of access programs can be questioned, as individuals from low-income families remain much less likely than their more affluent counterparts to participate in higher education.

Suppliers. The supply and production activities of colleges and universities have long been of interest to economists. Research on these topics proceeds along several fronts. For example, there are the traditional econometric studies of the production function (outputs as a function of inputs) and the cost function (costs as a function of outputs). The focus of these studies is resource use and cost behavior, particularly with respect to scale economies, the relationship between marginal and average costs, and the range of production possibilities given extant technology. Hopkins (1990) and Brinkman (1990) provide overviews of production and cost function analyses, respectively.

Not surprisingly, supplier pricing policies in higher education have been of interest recently. Winston (1996) looks at these policies as part of an analysis of subsidies in higher education (see also Rothschild and White, 1995). Reynolds (1998) discusses the role of student financial aid in price discrimination as practiced by colleges and universities. Berg and Hoenack (1987) explain how one institution developed a systematic link between tuition and the cost of instruction.

Closely aligned with an interest in pricing policies are studies of revenue flows into higher education and of how those revenues are used. Clotfelter (1996), Getz and Siegfried (1991), and Winston (1996) demonstrate a variety of uses of revenue and expenditure data, ranging from longitudinal and cross-sectional analyses by institutional type to detailed source-use matrices for individual institutions. James's analysis (1978) of cross-subsidies, wherein excess revenues generated by profitable activities are used to support or subsidize activities that do not cover their costs, is one of the most frequently cited articles in the economics of higher education. Bowen (1980) examines the relationship between institutional goals, revenue strategies, and costs. Massy (1996) examines resource allocation strategies designed to increase productivity in higher education, a familiar theme throughout the 1990s. Ehrenberg (1991) examines a key element in production costs, the supply of academic labor.

Most colleges and universities are nonprofit organizations. James (1990) and Winston (1996) discuss what that status means for their economic behavior. In general, the growing interest in nonprofit organizations is resulting in increasingly refined explanatory frameworks for understanding colleges and universities. Ehrenberg (1999) reflects on how a variety of economic concepts such as utility maximization, the appropriate response to changes in the relative prices among commodities, and the marginal utility of developing information on the cost of space may be applied to the management of colleges and universities.

Markets. The nature of the higher education market has been debated for some time. For example, it can be argued that the competitive market model is not appropriate to higher education because, among other reasons, students lack the knowledge required to be truly discriminating buyers. As Winston (1992) stresses, higher education is in reality a trust market, that is, a market in which the seller knows more than the buyer. Also, the higher education market doesn't clear in the usual sense, as a portion of it continues to have excess demand; in other words, selective colleges never do meet demand. Significant differences in supplier costs and a complex array of subsidies also set higher education apart from typical industries in the for-profit sector of the economy (Winston, 1996).

Investments. Higher education can be viewed as an investment at the individual and at the social level. Costs are important at both levels, as they would be in any investment decision. Students evaluate the cost of attendance against future income streams that may flow from that attendance. States and nations evaluate whether they may be spending too much or too little on higher education given its various social benefits.

Newspapers frequently cite reports from the U.S. Census Bureau on wage differentials between individuals with a college education and those without. Economists typically are more interested in the internal rate of return, which takes the cost of attending college into account as well as differences in wages or income; Paulsen (1998) summarizes research results as well as the underlying concepts. Generally, individual rates of return are quite competitive when compared with long-run returns from stocks and bonds, but they vary considerably by field of study, degree level, gender, and race (see Cooper and Cohn, 1997, for a recent analysis of returns by gender and race).

The monetary social return to higher education has been pursued along several lines. A comparison of total benefits received by individuals and society with total costs for higher education borne by individuals and society can yield a rate-of-return figure. Those rates fluctuate over time but, as in the case of individuals, they tend to be favorable when compared with investment benchmarks (McMahon, 1991). Another form of monetary social return is the impact that colleges and universities have on the local and regional economies in which they reside. Leslie and Slaughter (1992) compile the results of numerous studies of local impact, whereas Stokes and Coomes (1998) provide an overview of methods and practice. Higher education also has an effect on the national economy, including positive impacts on economic growth, productivity, unemployment rates, and business creation. Empirical studies attempting to measure this impact began in the 1960s. Becker and Lewis (1993) provide recent perspectives on this complex topic.

Benefits from investing in higher education are relevant to the question of who should pay for college. Economists address this question within the framework of welfare economics (not welfare in terms of payments to the poor but rather social welfare writ large) and public finance, wherein the focus is on appropriate uses of public resources. The analysis takes into account whether appropriate amounts of higher education will be produced by the private sector and, because students are coproducers of higher education, whether students will invest adequately in higher education given the benefits. One can assume that these issues will become increasingly complex if the for-profit component of higher education continues to grow. A classic approach to the question of who should pay can be found in the work of the Carnegie Commission on Higher Education (1973). Reynolds (1998) provides a contemporary view on this topic.

Perspectives on Cost

There are many kinds of costs (see Brinkman and Allen, 1986, for an extensive delineation and discussion). What follows are reflections on several issues that economists typically find interesting when analyzing supplier costs in higher education.

Opportunity Costs Versus Accounting Costs. Institutions normally have an abundance of internal accounting data but may overlook various opportunity, or true economic, costs, that is, the value of foregone alternatives.

Although opportunity costs are often difficult to determine, there is good reason to be concerned about them rather than to just assume that they are equal to accounting costs. For example, as Hoenack (1990) points out, opportunity costs experienced by faculty may be less than the administration is paying them for a particular service. It is reasonable to assume, as Hoenack argues, that individuals closest to the action will discover the most efficient production possibilities. It may be too expensive for the administration to gain the same level of understanding, to see the production function as it really is. As a result, the observed budgets may exceed the opportunity costs of faculty and other staff; in other words, accounting costs may not reflect the supplier's true costs but rather the level of funding the buyer is willing to provide. These excess funds, when they exist, provide for discretionary supplier activities, such as nonsponsored research in the case of an academic department. Buyers end up supporting activities that they might not choose to support if they had full knowledge.

Opportunity costs can also be greater than accounting costs. Perhaps the best example is the opportunity cost of capital investments, which are often ignored in higher education. As Winston (1993) has stressed, capital has two costs apart from the initial investment: depreciation and opportunity costs in the form of foregone income. Typically, the latter are much larger than the former, at least in the case of long-lived items such as buildings.

Does it matter if this particular opportunity cost is ignored? It does when there is a need to determine true economic cost, as is the case, for example, when the decision at hand is whether to construct a building using institutional funds, funds that would otherwise be producing a revenue flow. Similarly, when an institution borrows from its reserves, it makes sense to pay those loans back at market interest rates.

Direct Versus Indirect Costs. In conventional higher education accounting, *full costs* are a combination of direct and indirect costs. *Direct costs* are directly related to a cost objective. For example, expenditures for faculty salaries are a direct cost of instruction. *Indirect costs* (often called *overhead costs*) are not directly related to the cost objective but are part of the supportive environment in which it exists. For example, costs incurred in running the purchasing office or in maintaining physical facilities are indirect costs relative to instruction. Perhaps the best-known use of data on indirect costs is in recovering overhead expenditures related to research done for the federal government.

In determining costs, the prudent analyst will consider whether data on full costs are required. They almost always are when a new academic program is being proposed. There may be impacts on the library, for example, and nowadays on the need for technological support as well. Full costs may need to be assessed if the costing activity is meant to support a responsibility-centered approach to budgeting (Rooney, Borden, and Thomas, 1999).

It is not true, however, that full-cost data are necessarily better or more informative than direct-cost data. It depends on the question at hand and the issues being addressed. Data on direct costs are particularly useful for local managers because such costs are likely to be under their control. Even if correctly allocated, indirect costs can mask important and interesting differences in direct costs. For example, if an institution were interested in benchmarking the cost of student-recruiting activities against the costs of recruiting at comparable institutions, it might be better to compare direct costs. Likewise, the costs and productivity of similar academic departments are usually best compared on a direct-cost basis.

A problem in determining full costs is that the schemes used to allocate indirect costs are, if not arbitrary, at least imprecise. This remains stubbornly true even though the problem has been worked on for some time, including a national effort in the 1970s and early 1980s to develop appropriate procedures for full costing (National Association of College and University Business Officers-National Center for Higher Education Management Systems, 1977; Hyatt, 1983). Despite such efforts, making mistakes in allocating indirect costs is still easy. For example, it is a heroic assumption that library usage correlates well with student credit hours across all disciplines or that one square foot of space is necessarily worth as much as another. The analyst who does not accept these simplifying assumptions is left with having to actually measure the impact of a particular organization or activity on various support systems, a daunting and expensive task that might at some point still depend on arbitrary valuation of some facet of the production process. The allocation of indirect costs is addressed at length, with perhaps different conclusions, in Chapter Two.

Similarly, depending on the question at hand, including the cost of capital as either a direct or an indirect cost may be appropriate, for example, when calculating the share of supplier cost paid by students versus the share paid by state government. It might also be appropriate to include capital costs when comparing the cost of alternative, particularly electronic, modes of delivering instruction against that of traditional modes. Of course, allocating to instruction a portion of the cost of multiple-use assets such as transmitters, servers, fiber optics, and so on can be a daunting task, and distributing meet shares of traditional investments in bricks and mortar is not easy either. Ignoring capital costs is unwise, however, and there can be value in the costing exercise even if precision is unattainable (see Chapter Three for an extended discussion of capital costs).

Average Versus Marginal Costs. *Average cost* is total cost divided by the number of units produced. *Marginal cost* is the change in total cost associated with one additional unit produced. Average costs are featured in many higher education cost studies thanks in large part to the ease of calculation in most circumstances. Marginal costs usually must be estimated rather than calculated (see Allen and Brinkman, 1983).

If the objective is determining the cost of a contemplated increase in production, marginal costs are better guides than average costs. If one is contemplating an investment among alternatives, an estimate of average costs at mature levels of production may be the better guide.

Determining marginal costs per se is often difficult. A useful substitute is to distinguish fixed-cost from variable-cost components and then to treat average variable cost (total variable cost divided by output) as an estimate of marginal cost.

Determining Cost

Costs can be determined in many ways, but most cost-finding procedures fall within three large families: cost accounting, statistical estimation, and simulation modeling. These procedures are best seen as complementary. For example, statistical estimation is usually conducted using data derived from cost accounting procedures. The cost accounting data developed for the Delaware Study of Instructional Costs and Productivity (Middaugh, 1998–99) is a good example of data suitable for subsequent statistical, econometric type analyses.

Cost Accounting. In cost accounting, the simplest approach is a matter of bookkeeping wherein the direct costs incurred by cost or budget centers are measured by their actual or budgeted expenditures. From this auditable, straightforward starting point, the cost accounting approach often becomes more complex because of the need to allocate those expenditures, for example, in determining full costs.

Allocation can be difficult even when focusing solely on direct costs. Most academic as well as administrative or service units in higher education use at least some common inputs to produce multiple outputs. For example, faculty members generally teach at more than one level of instruction. If they do and if one is interested in determining costs by level of instruction, then allocation of faculty cost is unavoidable. In a cost accounting mode, this is done by either asking faculty members for a self-reported distribution of their time, asking department heads to estimate the distribution of faculty time, or imposing a priori cost-allocation ratios based on teaching patterns. None of those methods is foolproof.

Recently, attention has been directed toward the costing of activities. At a high level of aggregation, this is nothing new. Instruction, administration, and so on are activities, and a commonly accepted structure of accounts by activity or function has been in place in higher education since the late 1920s, albeit with some modification along the way. At present, however, the focus is on determining the cost of much more narrowly defined activities such as paying an invoice or recruiting a student (for example, see Gordon and Charles, 1997–98). Cost allocation is a critical component of this type of cost analysis, regardless of how the activities are defined. Over the years, the utility of federal statistics on higher education has suffered from the lack of fully standardized allocation routines across institutions.

Statistical Estimation.   There are two threads within the family of statistical approaches to cost estimation. Most often, various regression routines are used to estimate parameters that reflect average behavior. Much less frequently used are linear-programming techniques designed to estimate not average but relatively efficient behavior.

Typically, costs (total or average) are regressed on the number of students or credit hours in the form of a cost function. Likewise, the number of students or credit hours can be regressed on the number of faculty and other available input measures in the form of a production function. In either case, cross-sectional or time-series data or both can be used. The goal of such studies is to understand how average or marginal costs behave in response to changes in enrollment or credit-hour production. Generally similar approaches have been used over the years, but recently more emphasis has given to modeling the multiple outputs of higher education institutions and to using neutral functional forms (that is, forms that do not determine a priori the shape of the cost curves). Recent cost function studies can be found in de Groot, McMahon, and Volkwein (1991); Dundar and Lewis (1995); Gander (1995); and Toutkoushian (1999).

On occasion, a policy issue might be appropriately addressed by studies that focus on the most efficient behavior. Such studies usually employ linear-programming techniques or other procedures to compute a convex hull. At present, the most frequently used version of the linear-programming approach is data envelopment analysis. Sperry (1995) uses it to analyze the efficiency of academic anesthesiology departments.

Modeling. Simulation modeling leads to *synthetic, engineered,* or *constructed cost,* all more or less equivalent terms. This approach consists of decomposing a production process into its basic ingredients and then studying alternative ways of putting the pieces back together to achieve alternative levels of cost. The best-known early study of this type is the analysis of liberal arts education by Bowen and Douglass (1971). They considered various ways that class sizes, modes of instruction, and so on could be arranged to lower costs per student. Costs in medical education have been looked at in a similar fashion (Gonyea, 1978). More recently, Massy and Zemsky (1994) have used this approach to demonstrate how undergraduate education could be undertaken for less cost.

What Factors Influence Supplier Costs?

Much has been written and said about the reasons behind the relatively rapid increase in higher education supplier costs. What follows is not another attempt at explaining that phenomenon but rather a brief summary of such explanations organized around five themes: environmental conditions, the nature of the higher education industry, organizational tendencies, human tendencies, and institutional output and production technologies.

Environmental Conditions. Many aspects of the broad environment within which colleges and universities must operate have been identified as leading to higher costs per student: an environment dominated by science-based technologies that evolve rapidly, a wide range of students in terms of interests and preparation for college, an intrusive regulatory environment, a litigious society, a society with expansive expectations for higher education, and an economic marketplace that occasionally generates exceptionally high input costs (Brinkman, 1992). Recent examples of the latter include labor market shortages in business and computer professional fields and monopolistic market structures for scholarly journals. The environment is also characterized by extraordinary wealth and abundance. It may seem tautological, but it is a fundamental truth that higher education expenditures have risen because colleges and universities have had great success in raising revenue. Their ingenuity in that regard must be acknowledged, but revenues also depend on the wealth produced by the nation's economy. The robust stock market of the 1980s and 1990s is a case in point.

Nature of the Industry. The fact that higher education is a service industry has significant implications for its costs relative to the economy as a whole. Baumol and Blackman (1995) characterize higher education as an industry that is heavily dependent on people, many of whom are doing complex, nonrepetitive tasks. Services such as higher education are characterized by slow growth in productivity relative to other economic activities. The result is inevitable by virtue of the relationship between productivity and cost. Over time, higher education must become increasingly costly relative to the economy as a whole. As Reynolds (1998) notes, higher education costs have not increased more quickly than the services component of the CPI, but they have outpaced much slower growth in the cost of manufactured goods and thus have increased at an accelerated rate compared with the average for all costs.

Most higher education institutions are nonprofit organizations. This makes them revenue maximizers but not, as opposed to their for-profit counterparts, cost minimizers. According to Bowen's revenue theory of cost (1980), colleges and universities raise as much money as they can and spend as much money as they raise. Increases in cost per student are not only to be expected within that framework but also welcomed.

Organizational Tendencies. Factors that impact costs can also be found in the way that all organizations tend to operate. For example, the aggressive pursuit of revenue leads to resource dependency, that is, the ongoing need to marshal internal assets to cultivate and maintain sources of revenue (Leslie and Rhoades, 1995). Relative growth in the number of administrative staff, or *bureaucratic accretion,* may be explained in part as adaptation to complexity (Gumport and Pusser, 1995). Relying on resource allocation schemes that typically feature some form of incrementalism does little to foster cost control (Massy, 1996).

Human Tendencies. Human nature also influences supplier costs. Those costs rise because of, for example, administrators who tolerate and even promote costly, process-oriented decision making (Zemsky, 1990); faculty members who are too busy with other things to carry a reasonable teaching load (Zemsky, 1990); and administrators and faculty who together seek prestige above all else (Garvin, 1980), maintain unbridled aspirations (Clotfelter, 1996), and foster an extreme level of competitiveness within the industry (O'Keefe, 1987).

Institutional Output and Production Technologies. A traditional source of explanation for cost behavior is the nature of an organization's output. For example, enrollment in a college may shift toward more costly programs. Production technologies obviously are another important element in cost behavior. The incorporation of electronic information technologies in the instructional process may eventually help to contain costs, but thus far adopting those technologies typically has led to higher costs.

Conclusion

Costs in higher education, even when restricted to supplier costs, are not one thing but many. Consequently, the study of those costs has many dimensions. Calculating, estimating, or simulating those costs can be complicated. Explaining, justifying, or critiquing them is almost always complicated and sometimes controversial.

Notwithstanding the considerable effort and thought that has gone into understanding higher education costs, it would be difficult to overemphasize the importance of developing valid cost data at the appropriate level of analysis. Merely looking at changes in the bottom line is not sufficient, and neither is taking accounting categories such as institutional support at face value. It is critical to know what actually has been happening in some considerable detail. Perhaps the best recent example of this type of fact identification is Clotfelter's longitudinal study (1996) of expenditures at four institutions. More of these detailed analyses of expenditures would be helpful.

References

Allen, R., and Brinkman, P. *Marginal Costing Techniques for Higher Education.* Boulder, Colo.: National Center for Higher Education Management Systems, 1983.

Baumol, W., and Blackman, S.A.B. "How to Think About Rising College Costs." *Planning for Higher Education,* 1995, *23*(4), 1–7.

Becker, W. E., and Lewis, D. R. (eds.). *Higher Education and Economic Growth.* Boston: Kluwer, 1993.

Berg, D. J., and Hoenack, S. A. "The Concept of Cost-Related Tuition and Its Implementation at the University of Minnesota." *Journal of Higher Education,* 1987, *58*(3), 276–305.

Bowen, H. R. *The Cost of Higher Education: How Much Do Colleges and Universities Spend per Student and How Much Should They Spend?* San Francisco: Jossey-Bass, 1980.

Bowen, H. R., and Douglass, G. K. *Efficiency in Liberal Education.* New York: McGraw-Hill, 1971.

Brinkman, P. T. "Higher Education Cost Functions." In S. A. Hoenack and E. L. Collins (eds.), *The Economics of American Universities.* Albany, N.Y.: State University of New York Press, 1990.

Brinkman, P. T. "Factors That Influence Costs in Higher Education." In C. S. Hollins (ed.), *Containing Costs and Improving Productivity in Higher Education.* New Directions for Institutional Research, no. 75. San Francisco: Jossey-Bass, 1992.

Brinkman, P. T., and Allen, R. H. "Concepts of Cost and Cost Analysis for Higher Education." *AIR Professional File,* 1986, *23* (Spring), 1–8.

Carnegie Commission on Higher Education. *Who Pays? Who Benefits? Who Should Pay?* New York: McGraw-Hill, 1973.

Clotfelter, C. T. *Buying the Best: Cost Escalation in Elite Higher Education.* Princeton, N.J.: Princeton University Press, 1996.

Cooper, S. T., and Cohn, E. "Internal Rates of Return to College Education in the United States by Sex and Race." *Journal of Education Finance,* 1997, *23* (Summer), 101–133.

de Groot, H., McMahon, W. W., and Volkwein, J. F. "The Cost Structure of American Research Universities." *The Review of Economics and Statistics,* 1991, *73*(3), 424–431.

Dundar, H., and Lewis, D. R. "Departmental Productivity in American Universities: Economies of Scale and Scope." *Economics of Education Review,* 1995, *14*(2), 119–144.

Ehrenberg, R. G. "Academic Labor Supply." In C. T. Clotfelter, R. G. Ehrenberg, M. Getz, and J. J. Siegfried, *Economic Challenges in Higher Education.* Chicago: University of Chicago Press, 1991.

Ehrenberg, R. G. "Adam Smith Goes to College: An Economist Becomes an Academic Administrator." *Journal of Economic Perspectives,* 1999, *13*(1), 99–116.

Gander, J. P. "Academic Research and Teaching Productivities: A Case Study." *Technological Forecasting and Social Change,* 1995, *49*, 311–319.

Garvin, D. *The Economics of University Behavior.* New York: Academic Press, 1980.

Getz, M., and Siegfried, J. J. "Costs and Productivity in American Colleges and Universities." In C. T. Clotfelter, R. G. Ehrenberg, M. Getz, and J. J. Siegfried, *Economic Challenges in Higher Education.* Chicago: University of Chicago Press, 1991.

Gonyea, M. A. (ed.). *Analyzing and Constructing Cost.* New Directions for Institutional Research, no. 17. San Francisco: Jossey-Bass, 1978.

Gordon, G., and Charles, M. "Unraveling Higher Education's Costs." *Planning for Higher Education,* 1997–98, *26*(2), 24–26.

Gumport, P. J., and Pusser, B. "A Case of Bureaucratic Accretion: Context and Consequences." *Journal of Higher Education,* 1995, *66*(5), 493–520.

Hawkins, B. "The Confusing Economics of Higher Education." *Planning for Higher Education,* 1998, *26*(3), 8–13.

Heller, D. E. "Student Price Response in Higher Education: An Update to Leslie and Brinkman." *Journal of Higher Education,* 1997, *68*(6), 624–659.

Hoenack, S. A. "An Economist's Perspective on Costs Within Higher Education Institutions." In S. A. Hoenack and E. L. Collins (eds.), *The Economics of American Universities.* Albany, N.Y.: SUNY Press, 1990.

Hopkins, D.S.P. "The Higher Education Production Function: Theoretical Foundations and Empirical Findings." In S. A. Hoenack and E. L. Collins (eds.), *The Economics of American Universities.* Albany, N.Y.: SUNY Press, 1990.

Hyatt, J. A. "A Cost Accounting Handbook for Colleges and Universities." Washington, D.C.: National Association of College and University Business Officers, 1983.

James, E. "Product Mix and Cost Disaggregation: A Reinterpretation of the Economics of Higher Education." *Journal of Human Resources,* 1978, *13* (Spring), 157–186.

James, E. "Decision Processes and Priorities in Higher Education." In S. A. Hoenack and E. L. Collins (eds.), *The Economics of American Universities.* Albany, N.Y.: SUNY Press, 1990.

Leslie, L. L., and Rhoades, G. "Rising Administrative Costs: Seeking Explanations." *Journal of Higher Education,* 1995, *66*(2), 187–212.

Leslie, L. L., and Slaughter, S. A. "Higher Education and Regional Development." In W. E. Becker and D. R. Lewis (eds.), *The Economics of American Higher Education.* Boston: Kluwer, 1992.

Massy, W. F. (ed.). *Resource Allocation in Higher Education.* Ann Arbor: University of Michigan Press, 1996.

Massy, W. F., and Zemsky, R. "Faculty Discretionary Time: Departments and the 'Academic Ratchet.'" *Journal of Higher Education,* 1994, *65*(1), 1–23.

McMahon, W. W. "Relative Returns to Human and Physical Capital in the U.S. and Efficient Investment Strategies." *Economics of Education Review,* 1991, *10*(4), 283–296.

McPherson, M. S., and Shapiro, M. O. *The Student Aid Game.* Princeton, N.J.: Princeton University Press, 1997.

Middaugh, M. F. "How Much Do Faculty Really Teach?" *Planning for Higher Education,* 1998–99, *27*(2), 1–11.

National Association of College and University Business Officers-National Center for Higher Education Management Systems. *Procedures for Determining Historical Full Costs.* Technical Report no. 65. Boulder, Colo.: National Center for Higher Education Management Systems, 1977.

The National Commission on the Cost of Higher Education. *Straight Talk About College Costs and Prices.* Phoenix, Ariz.: Oryx Press, 1998.

O'Keefe, M. "Where Does the Money Really Go?" *Change,* 1987, *19*(6), 12–34.

Paulsen, M. B. "Recent Research on the Economics of Attending College." *Research in Higher Education,* 1998, *39*(4), 471–489.

Reynolds, A. "The Real Cost of Higher Education, Who Should Pay It and How?" In The National Commission on the Cost of Higher Education, *Straight Talk About College Costs and Prices.* Phoenix, Ariz.: Oryx Press, 1998.

Rooney, P. M., Borden, V.M.H., and Thomas, T. J. "How Much Does Instruction and Research Actually Cost?" *Planning for Higher Education,* 1999, 27(3), 42–54.

Rothschild, M., and White, L. J. "The Analytics of Pricing in Higher Education and Other Services in Which Customers Are Inputs." *Journal of Political Economy,* 1995, *103* (June), 573–686.

Sperry, R. J. "The Use of Data Envelopment Analysis to Study the Economic Efficiency of Academic Anesthesiology Departments." Unpublished doctoral dissertation, Department of Educational Administration, University of Utah, 1995.

Stokes, K., and Coomes, P. "The Local Economic Impact of Higher Education: An Overview of Methods and Practice." *AIR Professional File,* 1998, 67 (Spring), 1–14.

Toutkoushian, R. K. "The Value of Cost Functions for Policymaking and Institutional Research." *Research in Higher Education,* 1999, 40(1), 1–15.

Winston, G. C. "Hostility, Maximization, and the Public Trust: Economics and Higher Education." *Change,* 1992, 24(4), 20–27.

Winston, G. C. "Why Are Capital Costs Ignored by Nonprofit Organizations and What Are the Prospects for Change?" In M. S. McPherson, M. O. Shapiro, and G. C. Winston, *Paying the Piper: Productivity, Incentives, and Financing in U.S. Higher Education.* Ann Arbor: University of Michigan Press, 1993.

Winston, G. C. "The Economic Structure of Higher Education: Subsidies, Customer-Inputs, and Hierarchy." Williams Project on the Economics of Higher Education. Williamstown, Mass.: Williams College, DP-40, Nov. 1996.

Zemsky, R. (ed.). "The Lattice and the Ratchet." *Policy Perspectives,* 1990, 2(4), 1–4. Philadelphia: Pew Higher Education Research Program, University of Pennsylvania.

PAUL T. BRINKMAN *is associate vice president for budget and planning at the University of Utah.*

2

A common understanding of cost definitions is essential to creating reliable databases with optimal utility for interinstitutional analysis. Information provided by one institution must be compiled using the same rules as for that provided by peer institutions. Without this consistency, valid comparisons are not possible. This chapter will examine definitions of common expenditure categories, discuss cost-accumulation rules governing financial reporting, and examine the differences between direct costs of instruction and overhead or indirect costs.

Understanding Expenditure Data

Frances L. Dyke

Expenditure patterns are the cumulative result of decisions made about the utilization of institutional resources. They represent the outflow of resources to support the core activities around which colleges and universities are organized. These expenditures are accumulated into the broad functional categories of instruction, research, public service, academic support, institutional support, student aid, and operation and maintenance of plant. These general categories are defined independently of the source of funds providing support for these activities.

Costs accumulated in other functions such as auxiliary services are similarly categorized but are grouped according to both the source of funds (usually sales and services revenues) for activities not directly related to the primary institutional mission and the activities to which the costs are attributed. Common examples of auxiliary services are dormitories and housing, student unions, student health centers, and intercollegiate athletics. Auxiliary activities are considered self-supporting activities regardless of whether revenues cover expenditures. Hospital operations are classified in yet another category.

Understanding both the definitions of expenditure categories and the way to separate expenditures based on the source of funds is essential to accurate reporting, whether for internal or external uses. Institutions typically prepare financial information for a combination of compliance, management, and financial reporting. The underlying data are the same, but the decision rules on how to accumulate and categorize the expenditures may vary by the report's intended use.

Although management of the accounting and financial reporting systems is not the function of institutional research, a good understanding of the principles underlying cost accumulation is necessary before resulting data are used in analytical work. It is not necessary for the institutional researcher to become an expert in the principles underlying the concepts, but it is important to understand the framework and to become acquainted with the standard reference materials.

The National Association of College and University Business Officers (NACUBO) publishes accounting standards for educational institutions. These standards govern both the general-purpose financial statements and the accounting and reporting requirements for participants in federal programs. The standards for general-purpose financial statements have developed over several decades and have diverged for public and private institutions. The Financial Accounting Standards Board (FASB) sets accounting and financial standards for private institutions, and the Governmental Accounting Standards Board (GASB) sets them for public institutions. Additionally, American Institute of Certified Public Accountants (AICPA) audits, accounting guides, and statements of positions cover both types of institutions. Efforts are underway at the national level to develop reporting formats and standards that will bring more consistency to financial reporting for public and private institutions.

By considering the current Integrated Post Secondary Education Database (IPEDS) Finance Survey for public institutions, we can examine the key reporting categories relevant to understanding expenditure data. Having an example of this form before you may assist you in following the discussion. Alternatively, an outline of the major cost categories may also be found in Figure 5.2.

Current fund expenditures by function are reported in Part B of the IPEDS survey. Revenues supporting these expenditures come from tuition and fees; from state, federal, and local appropriations; and from gifts, grants, and contracts. Endowment income and sales and services revenues provide additional support.

Current funds are either unrestricted or restricted in their use. *Unrestricted funds* are available to the institution for any purpose within its defined missions. A governing body may decide that otherwise unrestricted funds should be designated for specific uses, but even under these circumstances the expenditures are reported in the unrestricted category. When an outside agency or donor constrains the use of certain funds, the funds are reported as *restricted funds,* based on conditions specified at the time they are awarded or donated. One of the most obvious examples of restricted funds is a federal research grant that supports specifically defined research activities. Another is a donation for scholarships.

Although the IPEDS Finance Survey, Schedule B, reports only expenditures from current funds, other fund groups exist to account for loans to students, faculty, and staff; for endowments; and for plant, agency, and other funds. Chapter Three will discuss how investment of plant funds is related to understanding the full cost of educational institutions. Otherwise, the reader is directed to the NACUBO and AICPA materials listed in the References for a detailed discussion of the remaining fund groups.

The total reported expenditures in each of the primary functional categories in educational and general funds may include the costs of personnel (salaries, wages, and benefits), services and supplies, and equipment. Identifying and accumulating these costs is the purpose of the institution's accounting system. Grouping these costs into functional categories is the role of financial reporting. Understanding and using both the financial reports and the information in the underlying accounting system is an increasingly essential skill as institutional researchers assist decision makers in achieving greater accountability in institutional performance. The Oregon University System has recently added a component to the evaluation process for institutional presidents that relates directly to the careful management of an institution's fund balance and requires that a target fund balance as a percent of revenue be set each year. This is just one of a larger set of performance measures for which presidents are held accountable and for which institutional research staff are expected to provide and analyze the data.

The following sections discuss the major functional expenditure categories, grouped according to whether the expenditures in the category are directly related to the core institutional mission or indirectly related to this mission of provision and dissemination of knowledge. Each section uses simple examples to explore some of the difficulties in assigning expenditures to these categories.

Instruction, Research, and Public Service as Direct Costs

The following section describes the functional categories for direct expenditures at a college or university. Precise definitions for *instruction, research,* and *service* are provided.

Instruction. Expenditures supporting the provision of instructional services are reported here. These include direct instructional costs such as teaching salaries and costs of instructional supplies as well as the costs of departmental support personnel and related office supplies. They do not include the costs of providing and maintaining the classroom space or of supporting central administrative offices or the library. Research and public service activities that are not separately budgeted and that may be supported by tuition and state appropriations (for public institutions) are also reported here.

Research. Expenditures for institutional activities designed to produce research results are reported in this category. Classification of these as restricted expenditures when they are supported by revenue from gifts, grants, and contracts is fairly straightforward. The difficulty often comes in deciding whether activities funded from unrestricted institutional funds are really separately budgeted research activities or simply part of the instructional budget. An example presented later will highlight the key decision points in making this separation.

Public Service. Colleges and universities typically offer a variety of services not directly related to providing instructional services and research outcomes. Although these activities may serve a training or informational function, they are not properly categorized as either instruction or research. Examples of these activities are agricultural extension services, conferences, broadcast stations, and similar activities that address local or state needs. Sometimes these activities are housed in separately budgeted administrative units; at other times they may operate from academic departments.

Understanding the Categories. The accounting and budgeting decisions controlling how these costs are accumulated are out of your hands as an institutional researcher. However, it is important to have sufficient understanding of the academic departments to differentiate subcategories of expense that represent a convenient bookkeeping convention from those that represent a separately budgeted item. Relying solely on the accounting title assigned to a cost category will not always lead to the right answer. Also, reports for different purposes may require differential treatment of the same items.

Example. The geological sciences department at Obsidian State University employs ten faculty and three office staff. In addition, three graduate teaching assistants teach one laboratory class each, and five graduate research assistants are paid from federal grant funds. The department delivers evening classes that are self-supporting and do not carry university credit. A government geologist who is not a regular faculty member teaches these classes. The department supports a speaker's bureau that regularly sends faculty and graduate students around the state to discuss landslide dangers. Office space is provided for all staff members, and a laser laboratory facility is available for both teaching and research. The department recently purchased equipment for three faculty members to use in field experiments and in laboratory courses. This department is the only occupant in its building, and the fourth floor houses a geological science library staffed by one librarian.

There are calculable costs associated with all these activities. The question is, Which of these should be reported as instructional costs and which as research or public service costs? At times the answers are not very transparent, and judgment tempered by a solid understanding of the academic environment is necessary. This judgment and understanding must be applied in the context in which the data are collected and in which the resulting information will be used.

Consider the different types of reporting mentioned in the introduction: compliance reporting, management information reporting, and general-purpose financial reporting. IPEDS represents a type of compliance reporting and collects aggregate financial data on the institution. Other studies such as the National Study of Instructional Costs and Productivity (the Delaware Study) discussed in Chapter Five collect data at the departmental level on direct instructional costs. It is likely that most institutions provide both mandated general-purpose financial statements and some combination of college and department- or discipline-level reports. One example of these department-level reports at Indiana University–Purdue University Indianapolis is described by Rooney, Borden, and Thomas (1999). Each of these data collection efforts has its own set of cost-accumulation rules that rely on the same underlying data but may produce very different ways of analyzing costs. Consider the example of the geological sciences department.

Expenditures for Faculty. First, consider the salaries and benefits paid for the ten faculty members. If all ten were appointed and continue to function as instructional faculty with responsibility for the generation and transmission of knowledge (the teaching, research, and public service missions of the university), then all salary and benefits paid from current unrestricted funds is instructional expense. This is true whether or not an individual faculty is teaching in a particular semester or term.

If two faculty members are appointed specifically for research and are separately budgeted as research faculty but paid by unrestricted funds, then the related salary and benefits are classified as research expenditures. However, if the two researchers are not separately budgeted, the related salary and benefits may be reported as research expenditures in one report (IPEDS) and as direct instructional expenditures in another (Delaware).

How is this possible? The unrestricted funds budget supporting instruction in the department includes the budget for the two research faculty. The department head and the dean have agreed that appointing two researchers in lieu of appointing two instructors strengthens the instructional mission of the department. Consistent with this decision, the researchers are not separately budgeted.

The accounting system codes the related salary and benefits expenditures as research expenditures even though the underlying source of funds is from the instructional budget. When the IPEDS report is prepared, these expenditures will be reported as part of the total for unrestricted research expenditures (dictated by the rules governing the accounting system). When a data submission is made for the Delaware Study, these expenditures will be reported as instructional expenditures (dictated by the rules governing the budgeting system). This is not a conflict. The IPEDS report will reflect the specific activity on which the funds were expended; the Delaware Study will reflect the expenditure of the total instructional funds available for discretionary departmental use to support its core instructional mission. This use of the funds represents a choice by the department to fund the two research positions to support this mission.

Next, think about the best way to categorize the expenses related to the evening class taught by the government field geologist. Again, we will see that these expenditures may be treated differently in different reports.

Because this is a self-supporting course that offers no credit, it is easily distinguishable from the regular departmental curriculum. However, it maintains the general characteristics of a course, and its expenditures are appropriately classified as instructional. The general instructions for completing the IPEDS Finance Survey state: "The instruction category includes general academic, occupational and vocational instruction, special session instruction, community education, preparatory and adult basic education, and remedial and tutorial instruction conducted by the teaching faculty for the institution's students." On the IPEDS financial report, the fees collected from the students will be reported as tuition and fees revenue, and the expenditures will be reported as unrestricted instructional expenditures.

These same expenditures will be treated differently in the Delaware Study and possibly in department-level reports prepared by individual institutions. In the former, the purpose of the study is to relate instructional costs to instructional productivity. One measure of productivity is the cost per student credit hour. Clearly, no credit hours are produced in the evening classes, which are self-supporting; the fees paid by the students are the only source of revenue covering the costs. And neither is any of the revenue from the fees used to support credit-bearing activity in the department. These expenditures would not be reported in the Delaware Study. Although they are direct instructional expenditures, they do not fall under the scope of the study, and including the data would skew the data for this department.

At the University of Oregon we prepare a department-level report of performance indicators. Included in this report on departmental activity and productivity are data on students and faculty, revenues, and expenditures. Although the expenditure data underlying the calculation of cost per student credit hour would not include the expenditure for the evening class as described earlier, a separate revenue line will show the revenue generated by this type of non-credit-bearing activity. This is one way to recognize the affiliated activities of the department without diluting the meaning of the standard ratios calculated across all departments.

Expenditures for Other Staff. The salaries of the three office staff are instructional expenditures if the primary responsibilities of these staff support the core activities of the department. Similarly, the salaries of the three teaching assistants are instructional expenditures. The reporting of these particular expenditures as instructional expense will not differ among the types of reports described previously.

The salaries of the five research assistants paid by federal grants are properly reported in all cases as research expenditures from restricted funds.

The total salary and benefits for the individual who is teaching only one semester is probably an instructional expenditure. However, if this individual is paid by a research grant during the time released from teaching, that portion of the salary and benefits will be reported as research expense from restricted funds.

Other Costs. The cost of maintaining office space for all staff members is not reportable as instructional cost and will be discussed in a later section on overhead costs. However, the cost of the office equipment and the cost of the laboratory equipment as described in the example will be reported as instructional expenditures. When equipment is purchased that can be used for both teaching and research, it is important to understand not only its primary use but also the amount of time involved in alternative uses. In this particular case, the primary use is teaching, and its use for separately funded research activities is incidental. For the purposes of financial reporting other than that specifically required for federal cost accounting purposes and compliance with Office of Management and Budget (OMB) Circular A-21 guidelines, attributing the cost to the primary use may be sufficient. Because this equipment was purchased from departmental resources that were not separately budgeted for research, the cost is reported as direct instructional expense in the Delaware Study. At the same time, the accounting system will probably support reporting a portion of the cost as research cost sharing for purposes of federal compliance reporting at a level of detail that normally will not be used by the institutional researcher.

The issues surrounding the expenditures for the laser laboratory also require some thought. Assume that the cost of the laser facility is substantial. If the facility is used heavily during the day for teaching activities and consistently on weekends and in the evening for separately budgeted research activities, it is important to allocate the associated costs for all reporting. If the accounting system does not support this cost allocation, then estimated usage should be determined through inquiry and an appropriate distribution of the cost made between the instruction and research functions.

The separately budgeted speaker's bureau represents a public service activity of the department. The only costs supported by this budget are the travel costs associated with speaking engagements and the cost of materials for presentations. No effort has been made to allocate a portion of the faculty or graduate student salaries, and none is needed. Only the travel and materials costs will be reported as public service expenditure in the reports described previously.

Organizational Support Expenditures as Indirect Costs

Indirect costs are those that are associated with activities that support the core functions of instruction, research, and service at a college or university. The following definitions apply.

Academic Support and Institutional Support. These two functions describe the majority of activities considered administrative in nature. Academic support activities relate directly to the instructional, research, and public service functions of the institution. These activities typically include deans' offices, other academic administration, libraries, museums, and academic computing and media support. Departmental administrative costs are reported as instructional expenditures and are not included here.

Institutional support activities relate to the more general, ongoing operations of the institution, except for the operation and maintenance of the physical plant, which is reported as a separate functional category. These activities include general administrative services such as payroll and other business services, human resource departments, and budgeting. They also include activities related to planning, legal services, and development activities.

Operation and Maintenance of Physical Plant. Expenditures related to the maintenance of the facilities and grounds used for activities supported by educational and general funds are accumulated in this category. All costs for staff, utilities, and other related services and supplies are included. When similar services are provided on behalf of auxiliary services and hospitals, they are not expensed here but in the proper auxiliary or hospital funds. Another group of funds called *plant funds* exists to record expenditures for the acquisition of physical properties, for renewal and replacement of facilities, and for retirement of indebtedness related to property acquisition and major improvements.

Student Services. These activities provide support services to students that are not directly related to instructional and research activities. Typically, these services relate to admissions, registration, and financial aid administration as well as to counseling, career guidance, and supplemental educational services such as tutoring and other academic assistance. Student services are often provided through student health centers, but expenditures for these will not be reported in the student services category if the student health center is organized as a self-supporting auxiliary activity. This is important to remember when comparing IPEDS information on student services expenditures across institutions. Sometimes a call to another institution is necessary to clarify the information and explain seeming differences in the proportion of current funds expended in different categories.

Applying Indirect Costs to the Instructional Function. It is always possible to consider the direct cost of instruction without recognizing any of the organizational support costs described by these four support functions. In fact, there is nothing wrong with doing so if the question under consideration is focused on the efficient use of funds budgeted at the departmental level.

However, to investigate the efficiency of the application of the educational and general funds available to the institution, a larger picture is needed. At a very basic level this may involve assigning these organizational support, or *overhead*, costs back to the instructional departments. The decisions on how to assign these costs will depend, among other factors, on the purpose for which the information will be used. It will also depend on an understanding of the cost drivers at the institution, the nature of the fixed and variable costs within the support services, and the other activities to which the same services apply resources.

Consider again the geological sciences department. So far we have reported only the direct expenditures of unrestricted funds to support the instruction, research, and public service mission of the department. We have not yet recognized the cost of the library (an academic support cost) or any of the costs related to the operation and maintenance of the facilities, the recruitment and registration of students, or payroll processing for the staff.

Activity-based costing gives us the tools to assign a portion of the organizational support costs to the academic departments. Utilization of these tools requires careful analysis of support costs before it is possible to make a reasonable allocation of these overhead expenses. A few simple examples will suffice to describe the underlying concepts. An examination of some of the issues surrounding allocation of operation and maintenance costs will demonstrate some of the complexities inherent in this approach.

The payroll department at Obsidian State ensures that all 220 university employees are paid at the scheduled times. Because the geological sciences department employs 22 of the 220 employees, an argument can be made that 10 percent of the costs of the payroll department should be attributed back to this instructional department. This is a simple and understandable way to allocate the costs. It is also a reasonable allocation scheme if the main cost drivers for the payroll department are the frequency of payroll runs and employee turnover, assuming that all university employees are paid on the same schedule and that employee turnover is consistent across campus. It may even be a good scheme when employees in different departments are paid on different schedules or when employee turnover is higher in some department than in others. This is because activity-based costing will not be an effective tool if the cost of maintaining the allocation system is too high relative to the benefit of the additional information gained or if it is too complex for decision makers to understand.

Another simple example is seen in an allocation of the costs of the registrar's office. Obsidian State has 5,000 full-time students taking courses for credit and no part-time students. The total amount of credit attached to student enrollments is 80,000 credit hours. The registrar's office manages registration and grading only for students enrolled in credit-bearing courses; an office for continuing education manages all other registration activity. The geological sciences department teaches 10,000 credit hours during the year. A simple allocation scheme attributes 12.5 percent of the registrar's costs to this instructional department.

In reality, of course, organizational support departments are not as simple as these are, and the activities underlying the costs may not be as easily identified. Time must be spent to understand the activities, their users, and their cost drivers before these overhead costs are assigned.

The issues surrounding decisions on the allocation of operations and maintenance costs provide an example of some of the more complex issues.

The geological sciences department is located in a new building with state-of-the-art offices and laboratories; it has an efficient heating, ventilating, and air-conditioning system, electronic locks, and a sophisticated security system. The history department is located in a building constructed in 1910 and renovated in 1952. The only ventilation in that building is from window fans provided by the occupants. The lighting is old, and there is no laboratory space of any kind because the closest computer labs for student use are in a neighboring building. Locks on both inside and outside doors are simple, and over the years many keys have been issued and not returned.

The facilities department provides utilities, maintenance, and security services for both these buildings. Activity costing requires that these costs be allocated as overhead to the user departments. Typically, operations and maintenance costs are a significant part of the institutional budget, and care must be taken in the allocation. Also, if the institution is a research university, some of these costs have already been allocated as overhead expenditures related to grants and contracts activities. This share of the costs cannot be reallocated back to instructional departments and must be subtracted from the total costs under consideration. At the same time, each of the cost components must be analyzed separately. For example, electrical utility costs may relate to the size of the spaces serviced, but they may also relate to equipment usage in those areas. If utilities are allocated as a fixed amount per square foot, the history department may be subsidizing electrical usage in the newer sciences building. Perhaps a more equitable and still simple scheme would be to determine one rate per square foot for buildings constructed prior to some year, say, 1970, and another for buildings constructed in that year or later. Alternatively, separate rates for science buildings and social sciences buildings could be determined.

Similar issues arise when allocating maintenance, repair, and security costs. Maintenance and repair costs may be lower in the first few years of a building's life cycle than in later years. Repair costs for certain systems may build to a peak level over time and then taper off. How can these costs be simply and reasonably allocated? A building with a sophisticated locking system may require less time from security personnel but more from maintenance personnel. Or it may require more security personnel because it houses expensive equipment.

As these issues demonstrate, developing an equitable overhead allocation scheme for management reporting is not a trivial exercise. Similar issues exist in the calculation of indirect cost rates to comply with OMB Circular A-21 governing recipients of certain federal funds. When indirect costs are identified for these purposes, they represent costs that cannot be directly traced to the specifically funded project but are realized because of activities that support the funded project. Examples of these activities include operations and maintenance, library, and administrative services. Although there is some complexity with assigning overhead costs, the discussion in

Chapter Three will show why this may be an important model to adopt when looking at the full cost of higher education.

Scholarships and Fellowships

Expenditures in this category are for outright grants to students in the form of scholarships and fellowships and are distinct from expenditures incurred for fee remissions for employees; recipients must be enrolled in formal course work and receive either tuition or fee remissions. For example, graduate students with appointments as teaching and research assistants may be exempt from paying instructional fees at an institution. This relationship is a bona fide employer-employee relationship in that work is required as a condition for the fee remission.

The expenditure for the fee remission is recorded as a fringe benefit in the department granting the waiver and is categorized as restricted or unrestricted according to the source of funds. If this is an academic department, it is likely that the expenditure should be recorded as a direct instructional or research expense. Similarly, when fees are remitted because of faculty or staff status, the remissions are also recorded as benefit expenditures and not as scholarship and fellowship expenditures.

Mandatory and Nonmandatory Transfers

Two other categories appear in various financial reports. *Mandatory transfers* from either unrestricted or restricted current funds to other fund groups are required transfers arising from legal agreements and grant agreements. These may include transfers for debt retirement, interest, and provision for renewal and replacements and matching obligations. *Nonmandatory transfers* are discretionary transfers from current funds to other fund groups or from other fund groups back to current funds.

Form Versus Substance

The ability of the institutional researcher to provide reliable, relevant, and timely information to institutional decision makers is enhanced by a solid understanding of fund groups, functional expenditure categories, and direct and indirect costs. The principles underlying the accumulation of accounting information are often complex, and the researcher's ability to use the information is enhanced through collaboration with staff in administrative and departmental offices. Sometimes looking only at the form of the information is not sufficient for a solid understanding of the substance of the information. This is particularly true when accounting systems must produce information that can be summarized for a variety of compliance, management information, and general-purpose financial reporting needs, each with a slightly different set of reporting rules. Having a clear understanding of the purposes for which information is collected as well as the instructions for recording the information is the only way to guarantee the provision of data that is comparable to that collected at other institutions.

References

American Institute of Certified Public Accountants. *Audits of Colleges and Universities, with Conforming Changes as of May 1, 1992.* Chicago: Commerce Clearing House, 1992.

National Association of College and University Business Officers. *Financial Accounting Manual for Higher Education.* Washington, D.C.: National Association of College and University Business Officers, 1990, with updates through 1999.

National Association of College and University Business Officers. *College and University Business Administration.* (5th ed.) Washington, D.C.: National Association of College and University Business Officers, 1992.

Rooney, P. M., Borden, V.M.H., and Thomas, T. J. "How Much Does Instruction and Research Really Cost?" *Planning for Higher Education,* 1999, 27(3), 42–54.

FRANCES L. DYKE *is associate vice-president for resource management at the University of Oregon.*

3

Full-cost models in higher education have long failed to account correctly for capital and financial aid expenditures. This chapter argues for a full accounting of all cost drivers that have an impact on expenditures in higher education.

A Guide to Measuring College Costs

Gordon C. Winston

In principle, measuring the average cost of providing a year of undergraduate education at a school is simple: add up its total undergraduate educational costs and divide by the number of undergraduates. But, in fact, several issues of concept and data make it anything but simple. Three things cause major problems: (1) the costs of using buildings, equipment, and land are both large (25 to 40 percent of total cost) and badly reported in college accounts; (2) it is not at all clear whether financial aid grants are a cost of education or a simple price discount (Bowen and Breneman, 1993; Rothschild and White, 1995; Winston, 1986); and (3) because colleges and especially universities do other things than educate undergraduates, major questions of cost allocation and joint costs have to be worked through to get to undergraduate costs. The capital cost and financial aid problems exist for all schools, whereas cost allocation is more a problem for complicated universities than for simple liberal arts colleges—in fact, Williams and Swarthmore and Carleton don't seem to have that problem at all.

The purpose of this chapter is to describe what has been learned in doing a fair amount of college cost estimation, both for individual schools from their own financial records and for the whole of higher education using U.S. Department of Education data from the Integrated Post Secondary Education Database (IPEDS) Finance Survey. Those estimates have both generated educational costs per se and provided a major raw material for the estimation of student subsidies. Many of the issues discussed here have been treated in greater detail in several discussion papers, and some subsequent publications, produced by the Williams Project on the Economics of Higher

Comments from Jared Carbone, Larry Litten, and James Roberts on an earlier draft were especially helpful.

Education (see Winston, 1992, 1993a, 1993b, 1993c, 1994, 1996; Lewis and Winston, 1997; Winston and Yen, 1995).

Conceptually, it is surprisingly complicated to compute these costs, especially for those well trained in college fund accounting who find themselves confronted with a new and unfamiliar mental model. To sort the issues out, I had to go back to first principles and the economists of the 1930s and 1950s who were working carefully through the fundamentals of economic information (accounting) for for-profit firms—to Sir John Hicks (1939) and Henry Simons and Trgve Havaalmo and others—and merge that knowledge with the insights of recent students of nonprofit firms such as Henry Hansmann (1986). And my earlier incarnation as a capital theorist, during which I fretted about the way we understand the role of physical capital in for-profit production, proved unexpectedly helpful.

There are two kinds of problems in calculating college costs—understanding a conceptual framework that is different from both the familiar accounting in for-profit firms and the fund accounting that is only now being abandoned in nonprofits and, more pragmatically, finding the numbers that can actually be used to measure costs. People who have tried to generate reliable figures have found an audience whose conceptual hang-ups create serious barriers to accepting their figures, especially those describing the costs of the services of buildings and equipment and land, of physical capital. As is so often the case in the economics of higher education, what is sensible to even well-informed people can be dead wrong, whereas what is accurate is counterintuitive. So it may be most helpful to the presentation of my argument if I first briefly lay out the ideas that inform the methodology and then the procedures for getting the numbers. As regards those ideas, I shall try to suggest a way to describe the issues that might help skeptics appreciate why an unfamiliar framing is necessary to calculate college costs. And I include Table 3.1, the Statements of Activities page from Williams College's 1996 *Financial Report,* and Table 3.2, a spreadsheet that uses those numbers to generate the appropriate per-student costs, to make the issues more concrete.

Current operating costs obviously capture much of what is relevant, so I shall start there. In even the simplest school, however, they have to be adjusted by removing costs that are irrelevant to education. Some such costs are clear cut, but some are not. It is necessary to decide whether so-called financial aid costs are relevant or not—whether they are really costs of educational production, as in our accounting conventions, or, as is increasingly popular, simply price discounts that have nothing to do with real educational production. Then there are the entries that capture bits and pieces of the costs of using capital—interest payments and depreciation—but do it so partially and inconsistently that it is best to replace them with coherent and consistent estimates of the current cost of using buildings and equipment and land. Though this will become a bit more complicated under the new accounting standards of the Financial Accounting Standards Board

(FASB 117), as noted later, it will still have to be done. Furthermore, some costs are typically included in operating costs—under operations and maintenance—that are legitimate educational costs, but they describe capital investment for the future rather than current costs for the present year. Then there are the complicated issues of how much of these total costs should be allocated to undergraduate education and how much to other activities and, finally, how many full time–equivalent (FTE) undergraduates there are in a school with a significant part-time enrollment.

Operating Costs

Three modifications are needed to adjust the total operating expenses line in Table 3.1. First, some entries need to be subtracted either because they are irrelevant to undergraduate education (life income payments, for instance) or because they are to be replaced by more careful calculations (depreciation and interest on indebtedness). Second, scholarships and fellowships raise the question of whether they are costs of education or a price discount. Third, reported costs of operation and maintenance of plant usually reflect some spending that is strictly an operating cost along with some that are, instead, a capital investment.

Irrelevant Expenditures and Those to Be Calculated More Carefully. Life income payments, as noted, have little to do with the current costs of producing education, however much they may serve its future financing. Similarly, interest on indebtedness is a matter of financial management (and a complicated and interesting one involving arbitrage income for wealthy institutions). To the extent that such interest charges represent part of the real cost of funds, or opportunity cost of physical capital that is a legitimate current cost of production, they are captured in the more systematic estimates of those capital service costs described later. Therefore, their partial reporting is eliminated from current costs to replace it with the complete estimate of capital costs described in the next section.

Scholarships and Fellowships. If a school uses financial aid grants to increase student demand and fill seats and beds, they are clearly a price discount and should be eliminated from costs and subtracted from gross tuition and fee revenue to reflect what the school actually earns in tuition and fees. Financial aid is not a cost. This is contrary, of course, to what college accounting does, which is to charge all students the full sticker price and then, in effect, hand some of them money with which to pay all or part of that charge. A car dealer, in contrast, sensibly recognizes as sales revenues only what he actually gets from his customers as sales revenues, after—that is, net of—any price-shading.

But for some schools, however, it is not that simple. Rothschild and White (1995) and Winston (1996) have recently argued that quality higher education operates in an environment where peer effects contribute importantly to a student's education: good students educate good students. In

**Table 3.1. Williams College Statements of Activities
for the Year Ended June 30, 1996**

	Unrestricted ($)	Temporarily Restricted ($)	Permanently Restricted ($)	Total ($)
Operating revenue, gains and other				
Student tuition and fees	41,042,563			41,042,563
Sales and services of educational departments	1,489,249			1,489,249
Auxiliary enterprises	15,196,359			15,196,359
Special-purpose grants expended	975,287			975,287
Gifts and grants	9,632,606	5,611,832		15,244,438
Investment income	17,161,361	2,707,613		19,868,974
Realized gains spent	3,139,440	126,328		3,265,768
Interest on loans receivable	8,926			8,926
Other	822,929			822,929
Net assets released from restrictions	10,956,056	(10,956,056)		0
Total operating revenue, gains, and other	100,424,776	(2,510,283)		97,914,493
Operating expenses and other				
Instructional research	25,524,118			25,524,118
Academic support	3,970,229			3,970,229
Student services	6,979,599			6,979,599
Institutional support	12,870,573			12,870,573
Operation and maintenance of plant	6,891,072			6,891,072
Scholarships and fellowships	9,099,760			9,099,760
Auxiliary enterprises	13,059,803			13,059,803
Interest on indebtedness	1,826,303			1,826,303
Depreciation	8,409,626			8,409,626
Life income payments	2,238,097			2,238,097
Other	151,359			151,359
Total operating expenses and other	91,020,539			91,020,539
Change in net assets from operating activities	9,404,237	(2,510,283)		6,893,954

those schools, therefore, financial aid is much like faculty salaries in that it pays for student quality, which is an input to educational production. To the extent that this is true, financial aid payments are indistinguishable from any other payment to a productive input such as heating oil or administrative or faculty salaries. Thus, fellowships and scholarships should be counted as a cost of education.

Unfortunately, either assessment of the true financial nature of scholarships and fellowships can be right, depending on the role that financial aid plays in the functioning of the school—they can represent a pure price discount, or they can be payment for a factor of production. For the IPEDS

Table 3.1. (*continued*)

	Unrestricted ($)	Temporarily Restricted ($)	Permanently Restricted ($)	Total ($)
Nonoperating				
Realized and unrealized gains on investments	7,063,520	53,096,489	3,076,958	63,236,967
Other losses	(191,558)			(191,558)
Present value of future life income fund payments	0	(683,903)	(763,464)	(1,447,367)
Life income and endowment gifts	0	1,168,100	1,975,473	3,143,573
Gifts further designated	(40,448)	(54,568)	95,106	0
Provision for loan guarantee	(8,500,000)			8,500,000
Change in net assets from nonoperating activities	(1,668,486)	53,526,118	4,383,983	56,241,615
Total change in net assets prior to cumulative effect of accounting changes	7,735,751	51,015,835	4,383,983	63,135,569
Cumulative effect of change in accounting principles		888,765	23,888,781	24,777,543
Total change in net assets	7,735,751	51,904,600	28,272,764	87,913,115
Beginning net assets	168,518,696	237,432,107	163,652,080	569,602,883
Ending net assets	176,254,447	289,336,707	191,924,844	657,515,998

Note: The accompanying notes are an integral part of these financial statements.

Finance Survey, which covers all sorts of schools, I have assumed that financial aid more often than not represents a price discount, so I have always subtracted it from legitimate educational costs, and I think that is probably the right thing to do. But among selective schools with long queues of applicants, financial aid improves the average quality of their students through the power of peer effects. In this case it can be considered a legitimate cost that buys an important input to their production of education. Note that treating financial aid as a cost of production also implies that grant aid is a legitimate income payment to the financial aid student—that he or she *earns* the financial aid by providing the college with something it uses in its production, whether it is work in the dining hall, linebacker talents, or the supply of peer quality. Under these circumstances, all students actually *do* pay the sticker price, partly in cash and partly in kind.

When in doubt, I would suggest calling financial aid a price discount and not a legitimate production cost. My reasons are timidity and a desire for uniformity—most schools use aid as a price discount, and until the recognition of peer inputs catches on, taking the latter approach will be hard to defend. Also, it is probably wise to save persuasive energy for the much more important issues of adequately accounting capital service costs. (And

Table 3.2. William College's Costs, Prices, and Subsidies: 1995–96

	Total ($)	Per Student ($) (N = 2,019)
Operating expenses		
Instructional and research (see note below)	25,524,118	12,642
Academic support	3,970,299	1,966
Student services	6,979,599	3,457
Institutional support	12,870,573	6,375
Operation and maintenance	6,891,072	3,413
Auxiliary enterprises	13,059,803	6,468
Total operating expenses	69,295,464	34,322
Scholarships and fellowships	9,099,760	4,507
Total operating expenses with aid	78,395,224	38,829
Capital service costs		
Replacement value	400,000,000	198,118
Deferred maintenance	12,000,000	5,944
Net replacement value	388,000,000	192,174
Depreciation (2.5 percent) on replacement	10,000,000	4,953
Opportunity cost on net replacement value:		
At 8.5%	32,980,000	16,335
At 12%	46,560,000	23,061
Capital service costs		
At 8.5%	42,980,000	21,288
At 12%	56,560,000	28,014
Cost: Aid as a price discount		
At 8.5%	112,275,464	55,609
At 12%	125,855,464	62,336
Cost: Aid as an educational cost		
At 8.5%	121,375,224	60,117
At 12%	134,955,224	66,843
Price		
Tuition, fees, and auxiliary	56,238,922	27,855
Scholarships and fellowships	9,099,760	4,507
Net price		23,348
Subsidy: Aid as a price discount		
At 8.5% opportunity cost		32,262
At 12% opportunity cost		38,988

Notes: Operation and maintenance have no renovation and repair component. Both reported depreciation and interest are replaced by capital cost estimates. An adjustment should have been made for $1,050,000 of funded research—trivial for Williams but serious for most universities. With that correction and with replacement value of capital reduced proportionately, cost and student subsidy would have been reduced by $963 or 1.5% and 2.4%, respectively.

because it does not matter to the calculation of subsidies whether financial aid is or is not added to both sides of the difference that defines them, I am particularly tempted to avoid the squabble.) It is important, though, to be clear and explicit and to report the size of financial aid, if it is included as a cost, so that others can subtract it for comparability.

Operation and Maintenance

Operation and maintenance of plant is reported as a current expenditure, and much of it is. But in many schools—beside things such as heating oil, janitorial service, and building management—it includes significant renovation-and-repair spending that offsets real depreciation and serves, therefore, the same long-term role as new capital investment. That amount reflecting renovation and repair should be subtracted from the year's operating costs and added, instead, to the year's new capital investment.

By consulting with facilities managers who can estimate how much of reported operations-and-maintenance spending is a genuine yearly operating cost and how much of it is a durable investment, the latter can be eliminated from current costs and added to capital investment. But without that information, no serious error is likely to be introduced by counting all operation and maintenance as a current educational cost because it is usually small relative to other costs. (The larger error, which can accumulate over time, will be found in the accounting of physical capital wealth alluded to later.)

The Cost of Using Physical Capital

This is the worst issue—conceptually and practically—in the calculation of educational costs because it is huge, and neither for-profit nor nonprofit accounting prepares us (or the critics) for its careful incorporation. Indeed, under the rules of fund accounting, financial accounts often described colleges and universities as if they taught their classes and held their labs outdoors in borrowed vacant lots and with no equipment—no recognition of the role or the cost of buildings and land and equipment was required. The new standards of FASB 117 that apply to private colleges and universities move in the right direction but not far enough to make the problem a trivial one. The neglect of capital distorts calculated educational costs by 25 to 40 percent.

All sorts of things mess up our understanding of the costs of capital services in production: unlike labor or office supplies that are bought from outsiders at a price, the services of buildings, equipment, and land often come from capital stocks owned by the college itself; capital is durable, purchased at a considerable cost in one year for use over future years; inflation changes the value of a building without regard to its condition or use or the services it yields; capital wears out through use and the elements and obsolescence, so its value depreciates over time without regular maintenance spending to offset it; and resources—funds—that have been devoted to buying physical capital are locked up and unavailable for a long time either for alternative uses or to earn a financial return. Finally, a careful accounting of capital costs and capital wealth is not necessary in the for-profit firms that dominate the economy because both returns to capital and returns to entrepreneurial risk taking are lumped together under what Economics 101 instructors take pains to call *accounting profits* and because a market in the firms themselves reflects the value of their physical assets.

Luckily, a lot of thoughtful attention was given to all this by earlier economists, even though little has made its way into college accounting conventions. However, that attention does give us a coherent basis for generating reasonable and consistent estimates of the costs of capital services in education. That they do not ring immediate and familiar bells makes it harder to gain acceptance for those estimates. (Or maybe it recommends some sensible vagueness as regards to what degree the costs of capital are estimates—see Carleton College, 1997.) They are, nonetheless, essential.

The value of the capital services used in production is unambiguously described by a *rental rate*—what a college would have to pay in a competitive market to use its buildings, land, and equipment for a year if they were owned by someone else. The components of the rental rate are (1) the current replacement value of the capital stock, (2) the real economic depreciation it suffers during the year, and (3) the opportunity cost of tying up resources in that form for the year. The rental rate, symbolically, is $P_kK(* + r)$, where P_kK is the current replacement value of K of capital stock, * is the yearly rate of depreciation, and r is the cost of funds, or opportunity cost, of tying up resources in the form of physical capital for the year.[1]

These three components of yearly capital costs can be estimated fairly reasonably and used to replace the partial accounting of capital costs reported in conventional financial statements (and IPEDS). So the procedure is (1) to eliminate from operating expenditures all reported values of depreciation and interest on indebtedness for buildings and (2) to replace them with a full yearly cost of capital services as a computed rental rate.

The Current Replacement Value of the Capital Stock

The major problem here, of course, is that accounting conventions report the value of a school's physical capital stock by adding together *historic* or *book values*—what each building or piece of land or equipment cost when it was originally purchased—with no attempt to account for changes in the prices of those things since then. The result is a jumble of costs of buildings and land and equipment, some reflecting prices prevailing in the 1890s, some from 1996, some from 1950, and so on. Every campus has its bizarre examples—at Williams a nice little faculty house with two bedrooms is carried on the books at $850 because that is what it cost to build early in the century. In book values, apples are added to oranges and flounder and new tires. Interestingly, of the two dozen or so financial statements I have looked at recently, Harvard remains the only school to report the *replacement* value of its capital stock.

Estimating replacement values for capital stocks to use as a substitute for the reported book values is fairly straightforward for an individual school. (And as with so much else in college's treatment of the costs of using capital, the present use of historical book values is so bad that estimates of replacement values can be pretty crude and still represent a major improvement.) Facilities managers can tap insurance records for current replacement values of buildings and equipment, and estimates can be made for replacement value of land and improvements. Some campuses have obtained engineering appraisals of replacement values. Consensus estimates of current replacement costs will generate usable numbers if all else fails. Updating these figures after one year's careful estimates can be done by tracking the value of new investment and changes in the construction price index. In the IPEDS Finance Survey, replacement values are requested and most schools do report, but for some it was necessary to estimate them from book values or educational and general (E&G) spending (again, details are reported in the Appendix to Winston, 1995).

Depreciation.   The idea that a capital stock is worn out by use, deteriorates through time, and loses value through obsolescence is not at all unusual, though the use of that fact as a vehicle for important tax advantages in business has pushed the measurement of depreciation pretty far away from its basic economic rationale. (Indeed, when I started out on all this ten years ago, I was told by a college comptroller that colleges did not have depreciation because they did not pay taxes.) But the FASB 117 accounting procedures take the important step of requiring colleges to estimate yearly depreciation and to include it as a cost of operation. The only problem remaining is that the *base* for that estimate is the highly understated book value of capital. Note that depreciation is intended to capture the actual decline in value during the year, absent maintenance spending, not the present value of anticipated possible future loss from events such as fires.

Depreciation is reflected in the rental rate as a yearly percentage of the replacement value of the capital stock. That rate can be developed from considerable detail, using different rates (useful life estimates) for different types of capital (see, for instance, Probasco, 1991), or it can be done more simply as an average over the aggregate of all of the school's capital. In both the individual school estimates shown in Tables 3.1 and 3.2 and those for IPEDS, I have used 2.5 percent of replacement value (from Dunn, 1989) and that, reassuringly, is just about what Harvard's very thoughtful procedure works out to be. Of course, a larger percentage rate can arbitrarily be applied to understated book values to back into much the same numbers—as Williams College seems to have done in 1996—but that procedure has little underlying rationale, and if it is right, it is lucky.

The Opportunity Cost of Capital

This is far and away the stickiest component of the idea that a rental rate measures the current cost of capital services. It will often prove as elusive or even counterintuitive to noneconomists in administrations and faculties as it does to Economics 101 students when they first meet the idea in fall semester. (An encouraging sign appears in "Lease a Computer?" (1998), where an opportunity cost is used explicitly—and identified as such—in an analysis of alternative ways to own or rent or buy a computer.) At base, it is pretty simple: the real resources—funds—that were used to build a building could be in use elsewhere if they weren't tied up there. Specifically, they could have been used to buy financial assets that would pay a yearly return: if you don't build a $1 million building, you've got $1 million to put into the stock market to earn (these days) $250,000 in the year. So if you *do* use it in the building, you have to recognize what you're giving up—the yearly earnings that that use precludes: $250,000. If you don't recognize that cost—if you recognize only depreciation costs—you're kidding yourself about the actual cost of using capital in education.

One thing we do not want to involve in the idea of opportunity cost is that it depends on who owns the capital stock—our measure of the cost of education should not be affected by ownership—yet conventional reporting leads to that mistake. Take two absolutely identical schools doing exactly the same thing, each with, say, $500 million in wealth. In one school, all that wealth is in the form of financial assets on which it earns an income that it uses to, among other things, rent its $250 million campus from somebody else. The other school has made a different portfolio decision—it has $250 million in financial assets and owns an identical $250 million campus. The costs of education in these two identical schools should be the same—and will be with an appropriate recognition of the opportunity cost of owning physical capital.

But, it might be objected, schools typically own part of their capital stock outright but have taken out loans against another part. That is why interest on indebtedness shows up as an operating cost in financial accounts. This fact has two consequences. One is that because the proportion of the capital stock against which debt has been issued will vary from one campus to another (and one set of state laws and agencies to another), comparability between schools—and for a single school over time—will best be served by replacing *all* such interest payments with consistently estimated opportunity costs. The other consequence is that for schools with endowments, borrowing is rarely necessary to finance building or equipment or land— the school could instead pay for it by reducing its endowment or quasi endowment. To do so, of course, would sacrifice returns on that financial wealth. If the school can borrow at a lower rate than the sacrificed earnings, it will be tempted to do so—simultaneously issuing debt and retaining financial assets in equal amount because what it pays in interest is less than what it earns. (Indeed, if the rate differential did not exist, it is not clear why a school would ever borrow, paying more on debt than it earns on the assets it protects by that borrowing.) So it seems wise to treat the interest on indebtedness, though nominally paying for the funds that built physical capital, as a strictly financial operation in which interest arbitrage earns revenues for the college—a transaction that has little to do with the actual costs of the use of capital. Interest, then, is fully recognized in the uniform opportunity cost of capital embedded in the calculated rental rate.

The procedural implication of all this is (1) to eliminate all interest on indebtedness from reported operating costs and (2) to choose an opportunity cost of capital that will form a reasonable basis of a calculated rental rate.

Conceptually, the right opportunity cost rate to use is the return the school would earn if its financial assets were greater. However, that rate—as the past few years have made very clear—is highly volatile over time as well as highly variable among alternative financial investments that differ in risk and return. So unless the purpose of the cost calculations is to track short-term changes, including those driven by the financial markets, a rate averaged over a long period makes the most sense. I have used, for the IPEDS data, a five-year average of the federal long-term bond rate—which came to 8.55 percent for the 1991 subsidy study—and for an individual school, a conservative smoothing of its endowment performance returns—12 percent for the Williams cost estimates in Table 3.2. To generate comparable figures for, say, the thirty-one selective private institutions in the Consortium on Financing Higher Education, agreement on something like a five- (or ten-) year average of the National Association of College and University Business Officer's reported endowment returns would produce uniformity and probably no more volatility than makes sense. What is important is that the chosen opportunity cost be (1) realistic in reflecting lost earning opportunities, (2) fairly stable if educational changes are to be tracked over time, and (3) consistent among schools if comparisons are to be made among them.

Note that even using something conservative such as the long-term U.S. bond rate, the opportunity cost contributes more than three times as much to the yearly cost of capital services as does depreciation. So the current practice in FASB 117 of including depreciation while excluding opportunity costs *seems* to recognize physical capital service costs but still seriously understates their contribution to college costs.

Furthermore, I understand that with next year's financial reports, FASB 117 will require that depreciation not be shown separately but rather embedded in the activities reported in current operating expenses. That will make it impossible to follow the procedure I have followed in the past—and recommended earlier—of subtracting those dubious depreciation estimates to replace them with the better ones just described. Nevertheless, there are some gains from this new procedure—at least part of capital costs will be allocated among activities, and it will still be possible to add in the larger and more important part of capital service cost as opportunity cost. So although $P_k K(* + r) = P_k K* + P_k Kr$ is the complete rental rate and the depreciation part, $P_k K*$, will be hidden in operating expenses, it will still be possible (and necessary) to recognize the larger part, $P_k Kr$, which is the opportunity cost.

In Table 3.2 I have done high and low estimates of the cost of a year of education, the low one treating financial aid as price discounting and taking the conservative opportunity cost of capital (to get a cost of $55,609 per student in 1995–96) and the high one treating financial aid as a cost of production and taking a 12 percent endowment return as the opportunity cost (to get $62,336). The difference is large, but both are a far cry from the $34,322 got by simply using E&G spending per student.

Two Further Complications: Collections and Accumulated Deferred Maintenance

Collections (and historic buildings) are quite difficult to value meaningfully and equally difficult to include in a blanket depreciation calculation. They do, typically, have a price and hence a replacement value (however appealing words such as *invaluable* and *irreplaceable* may be), but that value may appreciate with the passage of time rather than depreciate. The implication is that where they are a significant part of a school's wealth, collections and historic buildings may need to be recognized separately in replacement value estimates and in the depreciation component of rental rate. (In 1983, Williams completed its acquisition of supposedly irreplaceable original copies of the three primary documents of U.S. history—the Declaration of Independence, the Constitution, and the Bill of Rights—with the purchase, by an alumnus, of an original copy of the Declaration of Independence for $412,500. So even these documents have a calculable replacement value.)

The accumulation of deferred maintenance can be significant (Yale's announced $1 billion figure a few years ago made that dramatically clear), and it has implications for calculation of the rental rate because it reduces the opportunity cost associated with a given replacement value of capital stock. Letting maintenance go for a year frees up money that can be spent elsewhere, including investment in earning assets. Deferring a good deal of maintenance will free up a good deal of resources, reducing the opportunity cost of a capital stock of a given replacement value. (The Appendix to Winston and Lewis, 1997, spells this out more patiently.)

So the logic of opportunity cost applies not to the total replacement value of a capital stock but to its replacement value *net* of accumulated deferred maintenance. In estimating the rental rate, therefore, the solution is simply to apply the opportunity cost calculation only to the net replacement value while still calculating the depreciation component of the rental rate on gross replacement value. For some schools, this will make little difference in the year's capital costs; for some it will make a lot. (See note 1.)

Multiple Products, Cost Allocation, and Joint Costs

I do not have much that is useful to say about the issue of multiple products, cost allocation, or joint costs, not because it is unimportant but because its resolution is either terribly simple or terribly complicated and quite institution specific. Either way, no great generalizations seem to help.

The single product of liberal arts colleges such as Williams and Swarthmore and Carleton takes the form of undergraduate education, so, as noted earlier, it is safe to assume that virtually all current costs are incurred in production of that service. If resources are used for faculty research, for instance, they must be justified because of their effect—directly or through faculty engagement and recruiting—on the quality of the undergraduate learning experience. Pretty simple.

But even a relatively uncomplicated university has serious problems of cost accounting as it produces undergraduate, graduate, and professional education; health services; research; serious service activities; athletic entertainment and TV programming; and hotel and restaurant services. Costs have to be allocated among these activities, and joint costs have to be divided among them. This seems to be the most difficult problem facing the generation of meaningful estimates of the cost of undergraduate education in a university, and it is the problem most in need of coordination of methodologies and assumptions among schools if their results are to be comparable.

My own cost estimates have met this problem in the national IPEDS data used for subsidy estimates, but there I was precluded from a very sophisticated—and certainly an individually tailored—accommodation by the absence of data. Because there were no data on the differences in tuition and financial aid that would have been necessary to generate different subsidy estimates, I even ignored differences in costs by level of instruction. Inserting the Bowen (1980) cost weights (1.0 for freshmen and sophomores, 1.5 for upper-class undergraduates, 2.1 for first-year graduates, 2.5 for professional degree students, and 3.0 for advanced graduate students) without correction for tuition and financial aid altered the subsidy estimates by Carnegie classification but not in an unexpected way, so I dropped efforts to differentiate by level. On the other hand, I followed To (1987) in dividing aggregate E&G spending into (1) costs directly related to instruction; (2) costs irrelevant to instruction (graduate and undergraduate); and (3) joint costs, which I allocated on the basis of the relative dollar values of the other two. Capital costs were estimated for the whole of the institution and then allocated among functions (products) in the same way. Both of these procedures were, I think, defensible, given the minimal detail of national data, but neither would seem well advised for an individual university seeking comparability. If there is a cooperative initiative to measure undergraduate costs, this is surely the area where shared methodology would make the greatest contribution.

FTE Students

All of that estimated total undergraduate cost is divided by the number of students to get cost per student. Again, this is a simple procedure for Williams or Swarthmore, but it is not so simple for a university with more part-time students who make different demands on the educational resources and incur different costs. The conventional way to convert from part-time to FTE students is simply to assume that the average part-time student takes one-third as many courses and resources as the average full-time student, so one divides the number of part-time students by three to get an FTE figure. For IPEDS data, that is fine, but for any individual school with a nontrivial proportion of part-time students, it might make sense to be more careful in the conversion, using credit hours or courses or some other, more sensitive measure.

Subsidy Calculations

As noted a few times earlier, much of my effort on college cost estimates has been to generate meaningful figures for student subsidies—the average student's educational cost less the price that she pays, both net of grant aid. The total subsidy, in turn, is divided between a general subsidy that every student gets because her sticker price (gross tuition) is less than her educational costs, on the one hand, and any individual financial aid that further reduces the price she pays.[2] The subsidy calculations are indifferent (because of reporting and fungibility problems) to the source of the donative resources that support those subsidies.

Williams's Costs (and Prices and Subsidies) for 1995–96

The tables in this chapter show the calculation of cost (and subsidy) for Williams College. Table 3.1 reproduces page 8, Statements of Activities, from Williams's 1996 *Financial Report*, whereas Table 3.2 maps those data into a spreadsheet that adds capital costs and calculates the resulting educational cost per student. The simplicity that a single-product college allows will be the envy of those trying to allocate costs for a university, but the major issues of financial aid and capital costs—and their importance—are usefully illustrated, I think. I have calculated costs, as noted earlier, using high (12 percent opportunity cost and financial aid as a cost) and low estimates (8.5 percent opportunity cost and financial aid as a price discount). The mapping from financial statement to spreadsheet should be clear although, for reasons rehearsed at length previously, the replacement value of capital and deferred maintenance had to be estimated independently of the school's *Financial Report*.[3]

Conclusion

The purpose of this chapter has been to address some of the major issues involved in measuring the yearly cost of an undergraduate education as they have emerged in recent studies of colleges' student subsidies. Two of the three stickiest elements—the treatment of financial aid and of the costs of buildings, equipment, and land—have been addressed more successfully than the third—the less general problem of disentangling undergraduate costs within a university that does a whole lot of things other than teach undergraduates.

Notes

1. When deferred maintenance (DM) is considered, it is clear that with accumulated deferred maintenance, a year's rental rate is $P_kK^* + (P_kK - DM)r$ because past failure to spend to maintain the capital stock's replacement value has released funds for other uses, leaving only a net physical capital wealth, $P_kK - DM$, still tied up. But the whole of the capital stock, P_kK, nonetheless depreciates each year. See the Appendix of Winston and Yen (1995) on this.

2. Obviously (and conveniently), if financial aid is taken as a legitimate educational cost instead of a price discount, the difference that defines subsidy is unchanged as financial aid is added to both side of the equation $S = C - P_n = C + A - P_n + A$, where S is subsidy; C is cost without financial aid; A is financial aid; and P_n is net price or sticker price less aid.

3. And typical of the murkiness surrounding such estimates, the $400 million replacement value used there does not agree with a figure of $335 million in Williams's recent reaccreditation report. But, importantly, both are a good deal closer to the truth than the $134 million of book value reported in the *Financial Report*.

References

Bowen, H. R. *The Cost of Higher Education: How Much Do Colleges and Universities Spend per Student and How Much Should They Spend?* San Francisco: Jossey-Bass, 1980.

Bowen, W. G., and Breneman, D. "Student Aid: Price Discount or Education Investment?" *Brookings Review,* 1993, 11 (Winter), 28–31.

Carleton College. "Assuring Excellence." *Inside Carleton: News of the Assuring Excellence Campaign,* Summer 1997.

Dunn, J. A., Jr. *Financial Planning Guidelines for Facilities Renewal and Adaptation.* Ann Arbor: The Society for College and University Planning, 1989.

Hansmann, H. "The Role of Nonprofit Enterprise." In Susan Rose-Ackerman (ed.), *The Economics of Nonprofit Institutions.* New York: Oxford University Press, 1986.

Hicks, J. R. *Value and Capital: An Inquiry into Some Fundamental Principles of Economic Theory.* Oxford: Clarendon Press, 1939.

"Lease a Computer? A Closer Look at New Options." *Consumer Reports,* 1998, 63(2), 61.

Lewis, E. G., and Winston, G. C. "Subsidies, Costs, Tuition, and Aid in US Higher Education: 1986–87 to 1993–94." Williams Project on the Economics of Higher Education, Discussion Paper no. 41. Williamstown, Mass.: Williams Project on the Economics of Higher Education, 1997.

Probasco, J. "Crumbling Campuses: What Are the Real Costs?" *The NACUBO Business Officer,* 1991, 25(5), 48–51.

Rothschild, M., and White, L. J. "The Analytics of Pricing in Higher Education and Other Services in Which Customers Are Inputs." *Journal of Political Economy,* 1995, 103 (June), 573–586.

To, D. "Estimating the Cost of a Bachelor's Degree: An Institutional Cost Analysis." Washington, D.C.: Office of Educational Research and Improvement, U.S. Department of Education, March 1987.

Winston, G. C. "The Necessary Revolution in Financial Accounting." *Planning for Higher Education,* 1992, 20(4), 1–16.

Winston, G. C. "The Capital Cost Conundrum," *The NACUBO Business Officer,* June 1993a, pp. 22–27.

Winston, G. C. "Maintaining Collegiate Wealth: Global Accounts, Fund Accounting, and Rules of Thumb." Williams Project on the Economics of Higher Education, Discussion Paper no. 22. Williamstown, Mass.: Williams Project on the Economics of Higher Education, 1993b.

Winston, G. C. "New Dangers in Old Traditions: The Reporting of Economic Performance in Colleges and Universities." *Change,* 1993c, 25(1), 18–23.

Winston, G. C. "A Note on the Logic and Structure of Global Accounting." Williams Project on the Economics of Higher Education, Discussion Paper no. 23. Williamstown, Mass.: Williams Project on the Economics of Higher Education, 1994.

Winston, G. C. "The Economic Structure of Higher Education: Subsidies, Customer-Inputs, and Hierarchy." Williams Project on the Economics of Higher Education, Discussion Paper no. 40. Williamstown, Mass.: Williams Project on the Economics of Higher Education, 1996.

Winston, G. C., and Lewis, E. G. "Physical Capital and Capital Service Costs in U.S. Colleges and Universities: 1993." *Eastern Economic Journal,* 1997, 23(2), 165–189.

Winston, G. C., and Yen, I. C. "Costs, Prices, Subsidies, and Aid in U.S. Higher Education." The Williams Project on the Economics of Higher Education, Discussion Paper no. 32. Williamstown, Mass.: Williams Project on the Economics of Higher Education, 1995.

GORDON C. WINSTON is professor of economics at Williams College.

4

*Credible cost analysis on a campus entails careful
consensus building between and among both data
providers and data users. This chapter provides
practical suggestions for achieving that consensus.*

Building a Consistent and Reliable
Expenditure Database

Kelli J. Armstrong

In preparing to share data with others, be it on a single campus or across
multiple campuses, the following quotation comes to mind, attributed to
Sir Josiah Stamp of the British Inland Revenue Department in 1696: "The
Government are vary keen on amassing statistics. They collect them, add
them, raise them to the Nth power, take the cube root and prepare wonderful diagrams. But you must never forget that every one of these figures
comes in the first instance from the village watchman, who just puts down
what he damn pleases." Stamp's description of data sources is precisely what
we want to avoid when building databases related to cost and expenditure
information. These are the data that will ultimately be translated into information used for decision making at the most senior levels in campus and
system administrations. Perception of the data as unreliable or worse, whim-
sical, completely undermines their usefulness as a policy tool.

How, then, can a reliable set of cost data be constructed on a campus?
First and foremost, the data set must be created in a fully participatory fashion. The campus must not only know that expenditure data are available
but also believe the numbers. Believability can be achieved only through a
process that involves a broad spectrum of campus constituencies, that edu-
cates those constituencies on how the data will be used, and that steadfastly
adheres to the data conventions to which all involved have agreed. This
chapter will suggest broad process considerations for building a consistent,
reliable and therefore useful expenditure database.

Getting Started

For a discussion of expenditure data, we will focus primarily on costs at the unit level, that is, the academic department or the administrative office. The key here is to communicate data definitions and collection conventions in a meaningful way to individuals who may have little or no financial background. What do we mean by *object codes* and *function codes? Unrestricted* versus *restricted* funds? Although these issues may seem obvious to some of us in institutional research and have been clearly articulated in Frances L. Dyke's discussions in Chapter Two, many academic and administrative managers have only nominal familiarity with the basic constructs of cost data.

To help us in our mission of consistent reporting, it is important to underscore the fact that virtually all colleges and universities subscribe to the Generally Accepted Accounting Principles (GAAP), further delineated by the National Association of College and University Business Officers (NACUBO). Under these principles, every single business transaction at an institution is assigned a transaction number. Embedded in that transaction number is an object code and a function code. The sum of all of the financial transactions for an academic department or an administrative unit during a given fiscal year can be analyzed in a table that arrays expenditures by object and function, as is done in Table 4.1 for an undergraduate department in humanities at a major research university.

To examine cost data, it is important that unit managers understand the concept of expenditure objects and expenditure functions. *Expenditure objects* are those discrete categories that identify for what purpose funds were expended. The obvious object in most units at a college or university is salaries, as higher education is an extremely personnel-intensive industry. In the sample department in Table 4.1, salaries are broken down by personnel category—professionals, faculty, students, and so on. An object code is assigned to each category so that dollars expended for different types of personnel salary can be tracked. Similarly, object codes are assigned to nonpersonnel expenditure categories such as travel, supplies, equipment, and the like. The important feature in object codes is that they enable precise tracking of the various ways departments spend funds. *Expenditure functions* tell us just that—the organizational function for which funds are expended. In academic departments, for example, it is important to be able to distinguish between funds spent for instruction and those spent on research and public service. It is equally important at the institutional level to be able to distinguish between funds spent for academic support services and those spent for student support services. Function codes enable such distinctions. For example, in the department shown in Table 4.1, any expenditure transaction containing a function code between 01 and 08 is earmarked for instruction. Function codes between 21 and 39 identify those expenditures associated with research.

Using object codes and function codes, it is possible to determine that for the department in Table 4.1, a total of $27,735 was spent on supplies and expenses (discernable from object codes). Of the $27,735, $18,315 was spent

Table 4.1. Expenditures for an Undergraduate Department in Humanities by Object and Function

Expenditures	Instruction (01–08) ($)	Departmental Research (09) ($)	Research (21–39) ($)	Public Service (41–43) ($)
Salaries				
Professionals	26,509	0	0	0
Faculty				
Full-time (including department chair)	977,775	0	0	0
Part-time (including overload)	33,968	0	0	0
Graduate students	0	2,455	0	0
Postdoctoral fellows	0	10,321	2,591	0
Tuition/scholarship	0	6,122	0	0
Salaried/hourly staff	62,224	0	0	3,211
Fringe benefits	0	0	0	0
Subtotal	1,100,476	18,898	2,591	3,211
Support				
Miscellaneous wages	3,721	160	0	0
Travel	9,045	6,645	0	1,534
Supplies and expenses	18,315	6,860	2,560	845
Occupancy and maintenance	1,287	0	0	0
Equipment	0	0	0	0
Other expenses	9,083	0	0	0
Credits and transfers	0	0	0	0
Subtotal	41,451	13,665	2,560	2,379

for instructional purposes; $6,860, for departmentally sponsored research; and $2,560, for separately budgeted (most likely externally funded) research. The function codes identify the purposes for which funds are spent.

Institutional researchers and other analysts interested in this type of expenditure analysis would benefit by becoming fully acquainted with practices of staff in the campus business office. It is critical that the analyst understand the structure of the accounting system, including the conventions for assigning object and function codes. As a first step, the institutional research staff should meet with their counterparts in the business office to discuss the full file structure of the institutional accounting system. To best prepare for such a meeting, define precisely what the reporting requirements are ahead of time. For example, Table 4.1 can be replicated using SPSS or SAS report-writing capabilities. However, to do so, one must have a preconceived notion of the meaning behind the object categories and functional categories desired so that the business office can help to identify the appropriate codes to be used in the selection statements.

It is also extremely useful to work with the business office in developing appropriate backup data sources. Table 4.1 is, after all, a summary document and might be questioned by a unit manager. For example, an area of contention could be the $18,315 charged to supplies and expenses for instruction. An established working relationship between the research analyst and the business office might help the analyst produce a report that generates all of the transactions underlying that summary statistic. Often, once the summary statistic is challenged, further objections evaporate when the backup data demonstrate the accuracy of the summary report. A close collaboration between institutional research and the business office will help ensure the accuracy and effectiveness of expenditure data.

The other group of individuals with whom institutional researchers need to work closely are the unit managers themselves. It is important to run summary expenditure data (such as those in Table 4.1) by managers for verification purposes before incorporating them into any sort of cost or productivity analysis. A simple summary table is informative to the unit manager, both as a record of expenditures that he or she has incurred in a given fiscal year and as a basis for further analysis. The important principle here is to obtain agreement from a key constituent on the accuracy of the data. Campus seminars, workshops, meetings with chairs and department heads, or a host of other strategies are appropriate. Institutional researchers will want to involve campus constituencies actively in developing their own productivity metrics and supporting databases to reflect accurately their expenditures.

Pairing the Data with Output Measures: "Cost Per . . ."

Most institutions focus largely on what are termed education and general (E&G) expenditures. These refer to the cost of doing business in the central mission areas of a college or university—teaching, research, and service. They also include administrative and operational costs associated with those functions. Excluded are auxiliary, self-supporting operations (for example, residence halls, dining services, and bookstores). E&G expenditures affect the core areas of an institution and are those costs that merit the closest monitoring.

Table 4.2 reflects a fairly standard format for examining expenditure data over time and lends itself to some rather simplistic but useful analysis. For example, expenditures for instruction increased by 31.7 percent from fiscal year (FY) 1995 to FY 1999 at the institution depicted in Table 4.2; expenditures for student aid increased by a comparable 30.4 percent during the same period. Yet expenditures for institutional support (the accountant's euphemism for The Administration) increased by 60.6 percent during the same time frame. Such simple ratios might lead to larger underlying questions as to why these patterns have emerged. Viewed another way, institutional support as a proportion of total E&G expenditures increased from 7.5 percent in FY 1995 to 8.8 percent in FY 1999, while instruction as a proportion of E&G expenditures declined from 52.2 percent to 49.9 percent

**Table 4.2. Five-Year Trend in Education
and General Expenditures by Functional Category**

	FY 1995 ($)	FY 1996 ($)	FY 1997 ($)	FY 1998 ($)	FY 1999 ($)
Instruction	66,068,371	66,414,066	72,282,085	79,469,252	87,026,227
Research	12,866,345	14,122,085	14,990,564	18,860,451	19,134,857
Service	6,955,410	7,070,379	7,690,712	8,833,932	9,242,070
Academic support	6,693,753	7,239,802	8,426,643	9,387,419	11,704,716
Student services	5,993,236	6,170,383	6,642,681	6,954,039	7,350,709
Plant operation and maintenance	11,596,392	12,079,597	12,393,359	13,180,395	15,445,754
Institutional support	9,515,205	10,422,390	11,790,091	14,325,776	15,277,710

during the same time frame. Why the shift from spending on instruction to spending on administrative support programs?

Although these are valid and interesting policy questions, they are not terribly illuminating. Experience suggests that expenditure data take on substantially more impact when they are viewed within the context of some output measure: for example, direct instructional expenditures per student credit hour taught. Examined over time, the cost of delivering a student credit hour of instruction is far more instructive than simply looking at aggregate instructional dollars as displayed in Table 4.2.

It is important, however, to be careful and precise in choosing the variables in a cost-per type of analysis. For example, a number of institutions and agencies arrive at a cost-per-student ratio for describing instructional costs by simply taking the aggregate expenditures for instruction as depicted in Table 4.2 and dividing that by the institution's full time–equivalent (FTE) headcount. The result is an incredibly misleading number. Consider, if you will, a research university with a heavy curricular emphasis on graduate instruction in the physical sciences and engineering. Then consider another research university primarily concerned with undergraduate education in the humanities and social sciences. Using the cost-per-student formula previously described—totally insensitive to academic discipline and level of instruction—the former will appear substantially more expensive than the latter, despite the fact that there are good and valid underlying reasons why this would be so. Aggregate, institution-wide data are best used for in-house sorts of analyses such as those described earlier, when the disparity in growth rates between instruction and institutional support was noted. Interinstitutional comparisons are best made at the unit level, where contextual issues quickly become obvious.

In looking to academic and administrative managers for assistance in defining appropriate cost-productivity measures, it is important to involve them in the development of the databases from which those metrics will be derived. In Table 4.1, the importance of involving unit heads to verify the expenditure data was underscored. It is equally important to involve them in verifying those data that will constitute the denominators in any cost-per analysis.

The most appropriate denominators in ratios measuring instruction are cost per student credit hour and cost per FTE student taught. However, in this context *FTE students taught* does not mean the standard headcount measurement, wherein the number of part-time students is divided by three and added to the total of full-time students. Rather, *FTE students taught* is a derivative of student credit hours. It assumes that the typical full-time undergraduate carries an annual load of roughly thirty student credit hours per year, whereas eighteen would be the annual load for a full-time graduate student. These measures refer to semester calendar institutions; the respective measures would be forty-five and twenty-seven at quarter calendar institutions. The analyst then simply takes the total number of student credit hours generated at the undergraduate and graduate levels, respectively, and divides by the appropriate measure, as just described, to arrive at a figure for FTE students taught. This is a far more appropriate measure than headcount FTE. It provides a ratio of instructional dollars against a true output measure, the equivalent number of full-time students as measured by student credit-hour production. And it has the added advantage of being sensitive to the difference between undergraduate and graduate students. In calculating cost-per, the higher the number of graduate student credit hours or FTE students taught, the more expensive the program.

Because we are dealing with productivity measures that are derived from student credit hours, it is important that the number and type of student credit hours taught be carefully verified. In Chapter Six, David E. Hollowell and Melvyn D. Schiavelli provide a template (Table 6.1) for course verification that deals not only with the volume and type of student credit hours produced but also with the course type (lecture, lab, independent study) from which they were produced and the type of faculty teaching (tenured, nontenurable, adjunct, grad student). These are important contextual data. Courses taught primarily by tenured faculty cost more than those taught by adjuncts. Large group lecture sections are a more economical (although not always more effective) pedagogical delivery system than seminars or independent studies.

In verifying course data, department chairs should strive for optimal accuracy in the reporting of student credit hours. This means that they will have accounted for courses that might be anomalies, double counted, or in some other way inappropriately reported. These include

- *Team-taught courses*—assigning student credit hours to the department paying the instructor. If more than one department is involved, credit hours should be assigned in an appropriate proportion.
- *Dual-listed courses*—a single course section that is listed in the course catalogue with both undergraduate and graduate call letters.
- *Cross-listed courses*—a single course listed under the call letters of two or more departments.

Having taken care to involve the individual departments in the accuracy of both the unit-level expenditure and credit-hour data, it is possible to translate these measures into useful productivity measures, including

- Direct instructional expense per student credit hour taught
- Direct instructional expense per FTE student taught
- Direct research and service expenditures per FTE tenured or tenure-track faculty

Measures of this sort give a sense of return on investment and have power and credibility on campus because the appropriate affected constituencies have been involved in constructing the measures. In discussing expenditures, however, an additional word of caution to institutional researchers is in order. You will note that in the three measures just described, the expenditures are clearly identified as *direct expenditures*. Full-cost models are very difficult to develop, and the definitions for *indirect costs* (for example, administrative costs, utilities, plant costs, and so on) are as varied as the formulas for calculating them. The best strategy for institutional researchers in dealing with expenditure data is to keep the analysis as clean and straightforward as possible. By avoiding confusing terminology and ambiguous definitions, the credibility and understandability of the analysis is enhanced significantly (Stapleton and Lamangue, 1998).

What About Administrative Costs?

Reporting administrative expenditures is a bit more problematic than reporting expenditures for instruction, research, and public service. There is no uniform denominator such as a student credit hour, FTE student taught, or FTE tenured or tenure-track faculty. For functional areas such as admissions or purchasing, attempts have been made to analyze measures such as cost per admissions application processed or cost per purchase requisition processed. These efforts have achieved mixed success at best and do not readily lend themselves to interinstitutional comparisons. Some institutions are more technologically advanced than others and operate in a virtually paperless environment. Institutions that have been able to amortize technological costs and take full advantage of Web-based business applications clearly have a distinct advantage when it comes to cost containment.

In Chapter Five, Michael F. Middaugh discusses various ways in which expenditure data can be used and analyzed, focusing particularly on ratio analyses and on salary data as a major source of expenditure information. In the following chapter, David E. Hollowell and Melvyn D. Schiavelli discuss how expenditure data can lead to concrete policy change and innovation at an institution, specifically discussing student services and the impact of technology on the operation of a college or university. Although administrative data are more difficult to use in interinstitutional comparisons, those two chapters underscore the importance of maintaining solid institutional data on administrative expenditures and how those data can impact institutional policy and practice.

Conclusion

The present need for accurate, understandable, and credible expenditure data has never been more pressing. The U.S. Congress's frustration and dissatisfaction with rising tuition prices and the relationship to institutional expenditures led to the establishment of the National Commission on the Cost of Higher Education. The commission's report to Congress, in turn, has resulted in a mandatory study of the cost of higher education, whose methodology is currently under development through the National Center for Education Statistics. Institutional researchers can no longer remain detached or plead ignorance on issues related to financial matters. As the gatekeepers to campus information, they will be instrumental players in the analyses of revenue and expenditure data, not only for their own senior management but for external constituencies as well (Keller, 1993). Therefore, it is imperative that many of the strategies discussed in this chapter become part of the fabric of institutional research at colleges and universities. As institutional researchers take the lead to involve campus constituencies in the development of reliable and credible financial information, the confidence in those data will become infectious to those outside of the academy. We know that the central function of institutional research is to convert data into understandable and reliable information for policy decisions (Delaney, 1997). There are few areas as vitally important to campus and external constituencies as the management of institutional expenditures.

References

Delaney, A. M. "The Role of Institutional Research in Higher Education: Enabling Researchers to Meet New Challenges." *Research in Higher Education,* 1997, *938*(1), 1–16.

Keller, G. T. "Strategic Planning and Management in a Competitive Environment." In R. H. Glover and M. V. Krotseng (eds.), *Developing Executive Information Systems for Higher Education.* New Directions for Institutional Research, no. 77. San Francisco: Jossey-Bass, 1993.

Stapleton, L., and Lamangue, A. "Moving Beyond the 'Count'ing in Accountability: Creating Useable Management Information from Mandated State Reports on Faculty Accountability." Paper presented at the Association for Institutional Research, Orlando, Florida, 1998.

KELLI J. ARMSTRONG is director of institutional research at the University of Massachusetts system president's office.

5

*Once a campus has created a consistent and reliable cost
database, institutional data take on even more power
when they can be viewed within a comparative context
with other institutions. This chapter provides both
strategies and sources for comparative cost data.*

Using Comparative Cost Data

Michael F. Middaugh

As important as it is to develop a comprehensive database that contains reliable information about finances at a given institution, those data take on even more power and meaning when the information can be viewed against comparable data elements from peer institutions. Comparative financial data have long been available from a variety of sources and have been used—and misused—in support of policymaking at the institutional, state, and national levels. This chapter will examine interinstitutional data sharing and explore ways to optimize the value of information drawn therefrom.

Comparisons at the Institutional Level

The most comprehensive, public domain, comparative financial database is that derived from the Integrated Post Secondary Education Database (IPEDS) Finance Survey. This survey has historically collected data on current funds revenues by source and current funds expenditures by function as well as related data on salaries and benefits, financial aid, library materials, plant indebtedness, endowment, and so forth. Until recently, these data were provided in consistent format by virtually every college and university in the country and were available in computer-readable format from IPEDS or in ratio format from any of a number of commercial vendors, for example, KPMG Peat Marwick, Minter Associates, and so forth.

Ratio analysis (Turk, Prager, and others, 1995) is an extremely useful way to do broad-based comparisons of institutional finances between and among institutions. Perhaps the two most accessible types of ratios for those who do not have accounting or finance backgrounds are revenue contribution ratios and expenditure allocation ratios. Table 5.1 displays current fund revenues by source for a fictional institution, and Table 5.2 displays current

55

Table 5.1. Current Funds Revenues by Source

Tuition and fees	$88,150,000
Goverrnment appropriations	
Federal	2,500,000
State	63,300,000
Local	250,000
Government contracts and grants	
Federal	19,600,000
State	4,200,000
Local	150,000
Private gifts, contracts, and grants	11,150,000
Endowment income	21,250,000
Sales and services of educational activities	2,800,000
Auxiliary enterprises	37,300,000
Hospitals	0
Other sources	15,200,000
Independent operations	0
Total current funds revenues	$265,850,000

Table 5.2. Current Funds Expenditures by Function

Education and general	
Instruction	$105,950,000
Research	24,150,000
Public service	9,590,000
Academic support	13,700,000
Including library expenditures	8,800,000
Student services	9,300,000
Institutional support	22,400,000
Operation and maintenance of plant	16,200,000
Scholarships and fellowships	16,900,000
Mandatory transfers	3,710,000
Nonmandatory transfers	13,200,000
Total education and general expenditures and transfers	235,100,000
Auxiliary enterprises	35,200,000
Including mandatory transfers	2,210,000
Including nonmandatory transfers	1,530,000
Hospitals	0
Including mandatory transfers	0
Including nonmandatory transfers	0
Independent operations	0
Including mandatory transfers	0
Including nonmandatory transfers	0
Total current funds expenditures and transfers	$270,300,000

fund expenditures by function. Within the revenue contribution ratios, each of the revenue sources as listed in Table 5.1 is the numerator, whereas the constant denominator is the total education and general (E&G) expenditures figure displayed in Table 5.2.

The E&G expenditures figure reflects the cost of doing business at a college or university. It comprises total expenditures for the core functions of an institution and is net of self-supporting and auxiliary enterprises at the institution. The revenue contribution ratio for tuition and fees at the fictional institution in Table 5.1 would be $88,150,000 divided by $235,100,000, which is the total for E&G expenditures found in Table 5.2. The resultant ratio is 0.37; the ratio for state appropriations is $63,300,000 divided by $235,100,000, or 0.27. Each of the revenue contribution ratios reflects the relative importance of a given revenue stream to the expenses that they are intended to cover. The higher the ratio, the greater the relative importance of that particular revenue stream. Private institutions might use tuition and fees to calculate the relative tuition dependency of a given institution relative to a peer group, whereas public institutions might use state appropriations to gauge the relative level of governmental assistance within a group of comparable institutions.

Expenditure allocation ratios take a different view. Each of the expenditure functions—that is, instruction, research, public service, academic support, student services, student aid, institutional support, and so forth—are the numerators, whereas total E&G expenditures make up the constant denominator. The revenue allocation ratio for instruction in Table 5.2 is $105,950,000 divided by $235,100,000, or 0.45; the corresponding ratio for research is $24,150,000 divided by $235,100,000, or 0.10. Expenditure allocation ratios are a useful way of assessing the extent to which institutional expenditures reflect published mission statements. For example, the teaching institutions should show a relatively greater proportion of their total expenditures on instruction and academic support, whereas research and land-grant universities should reflect substantial proportional expenses in research and public service activities.

In making interinstitutional comparisons using ratio analysis, considerable care should be taken to ensure that peer institutions are using similar accounting standards.

Since 1995, there has been a dichotomous approach to accounting in higher education. The Financial Accounting Standards Board, which drives accounting at privately chartered, independent institutions, and the Governmental Accounting Standards Board, which oversees practices at public institutions, have taken distinctly different approaches with regard to the way in which tuition, financial aid, gifts, depreciation, and other financial entities are booked. Consequently, the ratio analyses just described are best analyzed when comparing similar institutions. At this point in time, it is difficult at best to compare revenue and expenditure ratios between Duke University and North Carolina State University, even though both are Carnegie

Research I institutions. A more appropriate comparison would be between Duke University and Vanderbilt University (both private) or between North Carolina State University and the University of Tennessee (both public).

Other forms of cost data at the institutional level are available, but they, too, have inherent difficulties. For example, average faculty salaries by rank are published by the American Association of University Professors (in the March-April issue of *Academe*), among others. Although average salaries at the institutional level are useful for analyses such as tracking annual salary increases over time, they are far less useful when one needs to determine market competitiveness within a specific discipline. For that purpose, data at the level of the academic discipline are absolutely essential. For example, the average salary for an assistant professor at the University of Delaware in 1997–98 was $48,400. On the other hand, the average university salary for an assistant professor in chemical engineering was $59,400, whereas the national and regional averages for assistant professor in chemical engineering were $55,670 and $57,757, respectively. The $48,400 university-wide average is of little informational value in trying to recruit a new assistant professor in chemical engineering.

For years, Oklahoma State University has published average salaries by rank for land-grant universities and has also done so at the level of academic discipline. Moreover, it provides the average salary for new assistant professors. All of the university's data on the subject is aggregated at the national level and by four geographic regions within the nation. A comparable analysis is provided for non-land-grant institutions by the College and University Personnel Association (CUPA). Representative data from the Oklahoma Salary Survey appears in Table 5.3. Consistent with the prior example, the data reflect salaries for the discipline of chemical engineering. CUPA Salary Survey data are formatted in similar fashion.

The data in Table 5.3 provide a wealth of information at a glance— mean, maximum, and minimum salary values; the sample *n* (NUM); and the number of institutions they represent (INS). These data are provided for the traditional tenure-track ranks as well as for new assistant professors. The analysis also provides comparable information for instructors and lecturers, although they are not displayed in Table 5.3, as well as a number of useful salary indices.

How can these data be used in comparative analyses at an institution? In addition to giving a department chair crucial information for recruiting new faculty, the data also show a given department's salary position relative to other departments at comparable institutions. Table 5.4 reflects the salary range for chemical engineering faculty at the University of Delaware and is extracted from a larger report that looks at all of the university's academic departments within the context of the Oklahoma Salary Survey data.

These data clearly demonstrate that university salaries in chemical engineering are highly attractive when compared with regional and national benchmarks and readily tell senior academic administrators what their mar-

Table 5.3. Salary Data from 1997–98 Oklahoma State University Faculty Salary Survey

Category: Engineering
Discipline: Chemical Engineering

	Full Professor			Associate Professor			Assistant Professor			New Assistant Professor		
	Salary	NUM	INS	Salary	NUM	INS	Salary	NUM	INS	Salary	NUM	INS
Average	$89,055	422	60	$64,376	187	57	$55,670	119	53	$52,112	12	10
High	$189,996			$96,000			$68,095			$65,000		
Low	$41,000			$45,730			$18,000			$46,125		
Faculty mix	57.3%			25.4%			16.2%			1.6%		

Table 5.4. University of Delaware Comparative Salary Data in Chemical Engineering

| | University of Delaware | | National | | Regional | | UD Department Average as Percent of | | |
| | | | | | | | Overall UD Average | National Average | Regional Average |
	Average $	n	Average $	n	Average $	n			
Full professor	117,757	15	89,055	422	97,379	139	129.5	125.5	114.8
Associate professor	73,451	4	64,376	187	67,827	62	120.1	114.1	108.3
Assistant professor	59,465	4	55,670	119	57,757	31	122.7	106.8	103.0

ket position is in terms of attracting and retaining chemical engineering faculty.

Comparisons at the Program Level: Academic Data

The foregoing discussion of salary expenditure data demonstrates the enhanced utility of cost data when they are examined at the level of the academic program. In general, cost data at the institutional level of aggregation have only limited value in understanding how costs can be assessed and contained. For example, a commonly used measure of instructional cost per student is derived by taking the total institutional expenditures for instruction as it appears on Part B of the IPEDS Finance Survey (Table 5.2) and dividing it by the total full time–equivalent (FTE) headcount at an institution. This is a very crude measure that allows only the broadest and most general comparison of costs between institutions. It makes no allowances whatsoever for the mix of disciplines that comprise the institution's curriculum, yet these very disciplines are often major cost drivers.

My own institution, the University of Delaware, comprises seven colleges. The College of Engineering and the College of Marine Studies are both laboratory and equipment intensive. Although the College of Engineering offers baccalaureate study, its international reputation comes largely from its graduate programs. The College of Marine Studies is exclusively graduate. Science curricula are frequently more expensive than humanities and social science curricula by orders of magnitude. Add to that the fact that graduate instruction is significantly more expensive than undergraduate instruction, and one sees that the aforementioned cost per student at the University of Delaware is quite misleading when compared with that of an institution whose curricula are dominated by disciplines that easily lend themselves to large-group, lecture-type instruction, that is, the humanities and social sciences.

It can be strongly argued that the most appropriate lens for making interinstitutional cost data comparisons is that of the academic program. The point will be illustrated by an extended discussion of the rationale, data definitions, and analytical conventions that drive the National Study of Instructional Costs and Productivity, or as it has come to be known, the Delaware Study.

When David E. Hollowell (who is a co-author of Chapter Six in this volume) arrived at the University of Delaware in 1988, my office was reorganized to report to him. One of the first major projects on which we embarked was development of a database that would contain appropriate measures of academic and administrative productivity and that would assist senior administrators in making resource allocation and reallocation decisions. This initiative proved prophetic; Delaware, like most of the rest of the eastern seaboard, experienced a significant economic recession in the early 1990s, and the database became an essential management tool.

The initial product of this database was what came to be known as the Budget Support Notebook. The notebook contained a series of indicators for every academic department or freestanding program to which faculty lines were budgeted. These indicators included

1. Degrees granted
2. Headcount majors
3. Student credit hours taught
4. Percent of student credit hours taught by tenured or tenure-track faculty
5. Percent of student credit hours taught by supplemental faculty
6. FTE students taught
7. FTE faculty, by category
8. Student credit hours taught by FTE faculty
9. FTE students taught by FTE faculty
10. Research expenditures per FTE tenured or tenure-track faculty
11. Public services expenditures per FTE tenured or tenure-track faculty
12. Direct instructional expenditures per student credit hour taught
13. Direct instructional expenditures per FTE student taught
14. Earned income from instruction
15. Earned income divided by the direct instructional expense ratio

The indicators in this list are self-evident and were described in detail in a chapter that David E. Hollowell and I wrote in a 1992 volume in the *New Directions for Institutional Research* series (Middaugh and Hollowell, 1992). The important feature of the Budget Support Notebooks, a sample of which is found in Table 5.5, is that they analyze teaching workload, instructional costs, and externally funded faculty productivity at the department or program level. They are responsive to the question, Who is teaching what to whom and at what cost? They enable comparisons between and among departments on a given campus with respect to the indicators identified previously.

As useful as these data are for comparing productivity and cost indicators on a given campus, they do not show where those indicators stand relative to academic programs or departments at comparable institutions. When the current president of the University of Delaware arrived in 1990, he wondered if it would be possible to get data comparable to our budget support indicators, and that request led to the development of the Delaware Study.

The first Delaware Study data collection took place in 1992. With funding in 1994 from the Teachers Insurance and Annuity Association–College Retirement Equities Fund Cooperative Research Grant Program and in 1995 through 1998 from the Fund for Improvement of Postsecondary Education, there have been five subsequent data collections. The Delaware Study has matured into a stable, sophisticated database that collects detailed information on teaching loads as well as academic- and fiscal-year departmental and program productivity. The study has profited from the conceptual and methodological wisdom of an advisory council composed of experts on faculty workload, cost and productivity analysis, and analytical methodologies that meets annually to refine and enhance the study's framework.

The Delaware Study now embraces nearly 300 participants who annually submit data by academic discipline related to

- Fall-term student credit-hour generation by level (lower division, upper division, and graduate) in both organized class sections and independent instruction
- Fall-term organized class sections—both credit bearing (lectures, seminars, and so forth) and those that are scheduled and for which attendance is a prerequisite to a passing grade (laboratories, discussions, recitations, and so forth)
- Fall-term student credit-hour and organized class section data, as described previously, disaggregated by faculty type—tenured or tenure-track, other regular faculty, supplemental faculty, and graduate teaching assistants
- Academic-year student credit-hour production, by level of instruction
- Fiscal-year expenditure data for instruction, research, and service

A sample data collection matrix is found in Figure 5.1 The data definitions, calculation conventions, and reporting options for the required data elements are fully described. Interested readers are directed to the Delaware Study Web site at http://www.udel.edu/IR or may simply write to me at the University of Delaware.

My provost, Melvyn D. Schiavelli, who co-authored Chapter Six in this volume, likes to focus on productivity from tenured and tenure-track faculty—and understandably so, as these faculty largely represent fixed costs, that is, they are permanently employed until retirement. The Delaware Study yields the following measures for him:

- Proportion of lower-division student credit hours taught by tenured and tenure-track faculty
- Proportion of lower-division organized class sections taught by tenured and tenure-track faculty
- Proportion of all undergraduate student credit hours taught by tenured and tenure-track faculty
- Proportion of all undergraduate organized class sections taught by tenured and tenure-track faculty
- Undergraduate student credit hours per FTE tenured or tenure-track faculty
- Undergraduate organized class sections per FTE tenured or tenure-track faculty
- Total student credit hours per FTE tenured or tenure-track faculty
- Total organized class sections per FTE tenured or tenure-track faculty
- Direct instructional expense per student credit hour taught

Table 5.5. Budget Support Data, 1995–96 through 1997–98

College of Arts and Sciences
Department X

A. Teaching workload data

	Fall 1995	Fall 1996	Fall 1997	Spring 1996	Spring 1997	Spring 1998
FTE majors						
Undergraduate	192	202	173	193	194	164
Graduate	25	27	27	24	26	27
Total	217	229	200	217	220	192
Degrees granted						
Bachelor's	—	—	—	—	—	—
Master's	—	—	—	—	—	—
Doctoral	—	—	—	—	—	—
Total	—	—	—	—	—	—
Student credit hours						
Lower division	2,825	2,909	2,185	3,049	3,239	2,450
Upper division	486	458	488	633	596	492
Graduate	246	161	240	147	166	184
Total	3,557	3,528	2,913	3,829	4,001	3,166
Percent of credit hours taught by faculty on appointment	98	96	95	100	99	99
Percent of credit hours taught by supplemental faculty	2	4	5	0	1	1
FTE students taught						
Lower division	188	194	146	203	216	166
Upper division	32	31	33	42	40	33
Graduate	27	18	27	16	18	20
Total	248	242	205	262	274	219
FTE faculty						
Department chair	1.0	1.0	1.0	1.0	1.0	1.0
Faculty on appointment	10.0	10.0	11.0	10.0	10.0	11.0
Supplemental faculty	0.3	0.6	0.8	0.0	0.7	0.2
Total	11.3	11.6	12.8	11.0	11.7	12.2
Workload ratios						
Student credit hours– FTE faculty	316.2	304.6	227.0	348.1	342.9	260.2
FTE students taught– FTE faculty	22.1	20.9	16.0	23.8	23.5	18.0

Table 5.5. (*continued*)

B. Fiscal data

	FY 1996 ($)	FY 1997 ($)	FY 1998 ($)
Research and service			
Research expenditures	364,517	314,502	264,032
Public service expenditures	0	0	0
Total sponsored research and service	364,517	364,517	264,023
Sponsored funds and FTE faculty on appointment	33,138	28,591	22,002
Cost of instruction			
Direct instructional expenditures	1,194,877	1,091,170	1,250,221
Direct expense per student credit hour	162	145	206
Direct expense per FTE student taught	2,344	2,113	2,984
Revenue measures			
Earned income from instruction	2,105,101	2,288,816	1,945,280
Ratio of earned income to direct instructional expense	1.76	2.10	1.56

- Direct, separately budgeted research and service expenditures per FTE tenured or tenure-track faculty

Figure 5.2 distills the essential data that the provost wants relative to tenured and tenure-track faculty into a single page. In assembling these data, it was important to choose a format that quickly and concisely communicated information and that readily captures the attention of a busy senior administrator. In the instance of Department X, it is readily apparent that although the cost per student credit hour is moderately higher than the national benchmark, the departmental teaching load and generation of external research funds are substantially higher than the national benchmark. These are crucial pieces of information in contemplating any resource allocation or reallocation decisions affecting Department X.

In doing comparative analyses such as that depicted in Figure 5.2, it is important to understand the strengths and weaknesses of the benchmark group. As a first cut in examining teaching loads and cost and productivity data at the University of Delaware, the provost likes to compare our data with those of research universities that submit data to the Delaware Study. His rationale is that because the University of Delaware is a Research II institution and because a significant number of the research universities in the Delaware Study participant pool are also land-grant flagship universities, in

Figure 5.1. 1998 National Study of Instructional Cost and Productivity

Institution:

Department/Discipline:

Associated CIP Identifier:

Please indicate the average number of degrees awarded in this discipline at each degree level over the three-year period from 1994–95 through 1996–1997.

Bachelor's:
Master's:
Doctoral:
Professional:

Place an X in the box below if this discipline is nondegree granting.

Place an X in the box below that describes your academic calendar:

Semester

Quarter

A. INSTRUCTIONAL COURSE LOAD: FALL SEMESTER, 1997

Please complete the following matrix, displaying student credit hours and organized class sections taught, by type of faculty and by level of instruction. Be sure to consult definitions before proceeding. Do not input data in shaded cells except for those mentioned in the important note below that pertains to (G) and (J).

Classification	Faculty			Student Credit Hours									Organized Class Sections			
	FTE Faculty													Other Section Types (Lecture, Seminar, etc.)		
	(A) Total	(B) Separately Budgeted	(C) Instructional	(D) Lower Div. OC*	(E) Upper Div. OC*	(F) Undergrad Indv. Instruct.	(G) Total Undergrad SCH	(H) Grad OC*	(I) Graduate Indv. Instruct.	(J) Total Graduate SCH	(K) Total Student Credit Hours	(L) Lab/Disc/ Rec. Sections	(M) Lower Div.	(N) Upper Div.	(O) Graduate	(P) Total
Regular faculty: Tenured or Tenure Eligible																
Other Regular Faculty																
Supplemental Faculty		NA														
Teaching Assistants: Credit-Bearing Courses		NA														
Non-Credit-Bearing Activity		NA		NA	NA	NA	NA	NA	NA	NA	NA					
TOTAL																

In the box to the right, indicate the number of graduate individualized instruction student credit hours from the total that are devoted to supervised doctoral dissertation.

Figure 5.1. (*continued*)

B. COST DATA: ACADEMIC AND FISCAL YEAR 1997–98

1. In the boxes below, enter the total number of student credit hours that were generated during academic year 1997-98 during terms that were supported by the department's instructional budget. (NOTE: Semester calendar institutions will typically report fall and spring student credit hours; quarter calendar institutions will usually report fall, winter, and spring student credit hours.)

A. Undergraduate

B. Graduate

2. In the boxes below, enter the total *direct* expenditures for instruction in FY 1997–98.

A. Salaries   Are the benefits included in the number reported for salaries (Y/N)?

B. Benefits   If the dollar value is not available, what percent of salary do
                     benefits constitute at your institution?

C. Other than personnel expenditures

D. Total

3. In the box below, enter total *direct* expenditures for separately budgeted research activity in FY 1997–98.

4. In the box below, enter total *direct* expenditures for separately budgeted public service activity in FY 1997–98.

Figure 5.2. Workload and Productivity Indicators—Department X

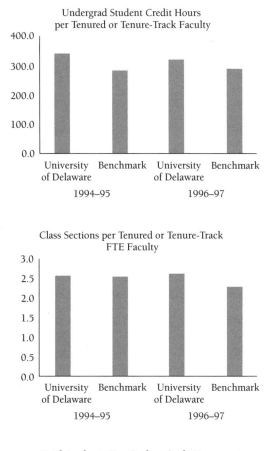

Undergrad Student Credit Hours
per Tenured or Tenure-Track Faculty

Class Sections per Tenured or Tenure-Track
FTE Faculty

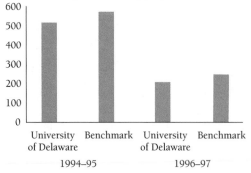

Total Academic Year Student Credit Hours
per FTE Faculty (All)

Figure 5.2. (*continued*)

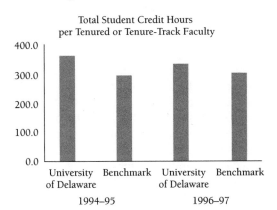

Total Student Credit Hours
per Tenured or Tenure-Track Faculty

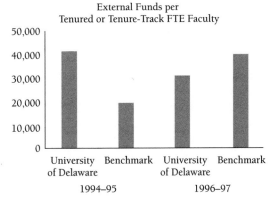

External Funds per
Tenured or Tenure-Track FTE Faculty

Direct Expense per
Student Credit Hour Taught

general they are the appropriate comparator pool. And in general, I agree with him. However, for our Philosophy Department, for example, research universities may well *not* be the appropriate comparators. The University of Delaware's Philosophy Department awards only the baccalaureate degree; those at other research universities typically house a master's program and frequently a doctoral program as well. Once graduate instruction is introduced into the equation, the teaching workload and cost factors change significantly, that is, to lighter loads and higher costs. Thus, it makes sense to compare the University of Delaware philosophy program to those at other institutions where only the baccalaureate is awarded. The Delaware Study affords participants that capability.

An additional consideration in making interinstitutional comparisons is ensuring that the benchmark data have been appropriately scrubbed. For example, in collecting data for the Delaware Study, it is essential that extreme measures not exert undue influence on the data pool. Consequently, in looking at a given variable, for example, direct instructional expense per student credit hour taught, an initial benchmark is calculated using all of the values submitted by a group of institutions for that variable. Then, those values that are more than two standard deviations above or below that initial mean are identified as outliers and are excluded from recalculation of a refined benchmark, which is subsequently distributed to participating institutions. In using comparative data, it is important to know what the mean, or benchmark, represents. How many institutions are taken into account? How many outliers were excluded? What were the criteria for exclusion? What are the maximum, minimum, and median values in the original distribution of response values? The more you know about the response pool, the more effective and informative the comparative analyses will be.

Clear and precise presentation of comparative data are important. When choosing the Delaware Study data shown in Figure 5.2 that I gave the provost, I was attempting to depict data from two separate annual data collection cycles and to compare them with the respective benchmarks for the year in question. This would give the provost a sense as to whether the data for a given year were idiosyncratic or part of an emerging pattern. Obviously, even two years do not constitute a pattern, but with each additional iteration of the *Delaware Study,* the data become more useful as a component in a time series. This rationale holds for any comparative data pool—it is best to examine data over time to see if there are discernable patterns. Readers interested in pursuing further uses of Delaware Study data are encouraged to read the two articles I wrote for *Planning for Higher Education* (Middaugh, 1996, 1999).

Comparisons at the Program Level: Administrative Data

It has been my experience over the years that solid external benchmarking data for administrative cost and productivity measures are considerably more difficult to acquire than academic benchmarks. The National Association of College and University Business Officers Benchmarking Project was a noble attempt at building such a database, but it simply did not meet the information needs of senior administrators on my campus. The measures were frequently too mechanical and inappropriate, for example, measuring admissions or registration activity solely in terms of numbers of transactions without any reference to quality or customer satisfaction. Comparative administrative data at the University of Delaware has largely focused on interdepartmental measures.

That is not to say that some useful external measures do not exist. We annually make use of both the CUPA Annual Administrative Compensation Survey (which focuses on essentially senior-level positions, that is, deans, directors, and higher) and the CUPA Mid-Level Administrative/Professional Salary Survey for examining the market competitiveness of our nonfaculty positions. CUPA (http://www.cupa.org) provides national and regional data for most administrative job titles at any college or university. For a fee, it also provides a customized salary comparison for our institution compared with the twenty-four peers with which we routinely compare ourselves for faculty and professional compensation purposes. Similarly, we obtain useful information on facilities space and staffing benchmarks from the Association of Physical Plant Administrators (http://www.appa.org). EDUCAUSE (http://www.educause.edu) is a source for data on computing practices. In short, those seeking external benchmarking data for administrative purposes are encouraged to pursue the matter with the professional society or association related to that particular institutional function.

Barbara Taylor and William Massy (1996) have written a valuable book, *Strategic Indicators for Higher Education,* that suggests a broad spectrum of benchmarks that measure overall institutional vitality and effectiveness. In looking at interinstitutional comparisons, the authors propose data sources that are, in large part, in the public domain, for example, IPEDS. Although providing broad indicators at the institutional level that are useful in framing general policy questions, the measures do not provide programmatic measures that focus on cost and productivity issues and enable managers to make better decisions.

Internal comparative data are more frequently used at my institution in examining issues of administrative cost and productivity. During the economic recession of the early 1990s, the Office of Institutional Research and Planning developed a report that looked at basic budget expenditures and positions principally funded from institutional sources. Table 5.6, which contains fictitious data, is a summary of the information provided in the full report. There, data are broken out by department or unit within vice presidential reporting area, for example, academic affairs, student affairs, administration, human resources, and so on. A similar report is also produced that displays basic budget expenditures, by unit, in terms of absolute basic budget dollars. By *basic budget,* we are referring to unrestricted institutional resources, that is, those dollars over which the university has complete discretionary authority.

Table 5.6. Comparison of Authorized Full-Time Equivalent Positions, 1993–94, 1997–98, and 1998–99, Basic Budget Only

	1993–94 No. of FTEs	1997–98 No. of FTEs	Net Gain (Loss) 1994–1998 No. of FTEs	1997–98 No. of FTEs	Net Gain (Loss) 1998–1999 No. of FTEs	Growth Index
All academic units	1,650.5	1,710.2	59.7	1,718.0	7.8	1.04
All administrative units	875.2	885.7	10.5	888.8	3.1	1.02
University grand total	2,525.7	2,595.9	70.2	2,606.8	10.9	1.03

These analyses are useful as they compare the relative growth of academic versus administrative functions on campus. Are administrative personnel increasing at a rate faster than that of academic personnel, as is the popular perception among many outside of higher education? This analysis enables the university to demonstrate that the growth of administrative personnel for whom it pays with institutional resources is lower than the growth of academic personnel. A sidebar analysis using the university's accounting system demonstrated that many of the new, supposedly administrative positions that appeared in the 1980s and 1990s were actually soft-funded grant positions associated with the institution's research mission and were not administrators at all.

Further analysis of the full report allows senior administrators to examine the growth rate in an area such as student affairs and to determine if it is sensible and consistent with the growth patterns in student enrollment. Or one can study an academic support area such as the library, which has been transformed by technology in the last decade, and see if personnel reflect that transformation. In short, these sorts of analyses, although interdepartmental within the institution, have enormous explanatory and decision support capabilities.

Political Considerations in Using Comparative Data

Although the foregoing discussion of comparative data analyses underscores the utility of understanding one's position relative to others, the individual using comparative data should understand that few other types of information are as potentially threatening to institutions and those who manage them. When we first began developing our Budget Support Notebooks at the University of Delaware, the general perception among academic departments was that the data would be used to deprive them of resources. The knowledge that we were developing the Delaware Study of Instructional Costs and Productivity initially brought comparable assertions that departmental productivity comparisons are not meaningful.

If comparative data, whether intra- or interinstitutional, are to be used effectively for policymaking and decision making, they must be the result of a collaborative effort between those who collect the data and those whose organizational units are most likely to be affected by the information. As both the Budget Support Notebooks and the Delaware Study evolved, we were very careful to include deans, department chairs, and representative faculty groups in discussions about the projects. We clearly explained data sources, definitions, calculation conventions, and the purposes for which the data were to be used.

At the University of Delaware, we assure data consumers that information gathered through comparative analyses in a single year will not be used to reward or punish a unit but will be viewed as longitudinal data over a multiple-year time frame as a tool of inquiry to develop explanatory frameworks as to why Delaware's data are similar to or different from national benchmarks. For example, the departmental data in any given Budget Support Notebook or Delaware Study cycle might be significantly affected by faculty sabbaticals or a major noncapital equipment purchase that might have the effect of lower productivity measures or higher cost indicators. These data are most useful when viewed over time for discernible patterns. That said, quantitative trend data, coupled with qualitative information provided to us by departments and programs, provide the basis for resource allocation and reallocation decisions at the University.

Some states and institutions are not so fortunate as my own, and comparative data may be used to develop indicators for formula funding. In those instances, it is particularly incumbent upon the institutional research office, as the data collector, to communicate clearly and succinctly to affected units precisely how the data are to be analyzed and the purposes for which they are to be used. Effective communication can lead to revision and enhancement of measures and to better data for better decisions.

References

American Association of University Professors. "The Annual Report on the Economic Status of the Profession." *Academe (Bulletin of the American Association of University Professors)* Annual March/April Salary Issue. Washington, D.C.: American Association of University Professors.

College and University Personnel Association. *Annual Administrative Compensation Survey and Annual Mid-Level Administrative/Professional Salary Survey.* Washington, D.C.: College and University Personnel Association.

Middaugh, M. F. "Closing In on Faculty Productivity." *Planning for Higher Education,* 1996, 24(2), 1–12.

Middaugh, M. F. "How Much Do Faculty Really Teach?" *Planning for Higher Education,* 1999, 27(2), 1–11.

Middaugh, M. F., and Hollowell, D. E. "Examining Academic and Administrative Productivity Measures." In C. S. Hollins (ed.), *Containing Costs and Improving Productivity in Higher Education.* New Directions for Institutional Research, no. 75. San Francisco: Jossey-Bass, 1992.

Office of Planning, Budget, and Institutional Research, Oklahoma State University. Annual Faculty Salary Survey of Institutions Belonging to National Association of State Universities and Land Grant Colleges. Stillwater, Oklahoma: Office of Planning, Budget, and Institutional Research, Oklahoma State University.

Taylor, B. E., and Massy, W. E. *Strategic Indicators for Higher Education.* Princeton, N.J.: Peterson's, 1996.

Turk, F. J., Prager, F. J., et al. *Ratio Analysis in Higher Education.* (3rd ed.) New York: KMPG Peat Marwick, 1995.

MICHAEL F. MIDDAUGH *is assistant vice president for institutional research and planning at the University of Delaware.*

6

Cost data are valuable only when they are used for decision making and policy development. Two senior campus administrators provide valuable insight into what sorts of data are needed for those purposes.

The Importance of Cost Data: A View from the Top

David E. Hollowell, Melvyn D. Schiavelli

The University of Delaware has always been a data-rich institution. Since the early 1970s, its student, personnel, and financial systems have contained data elements on virtually every imaginable variable. But the culture of sharing data as the informational basis for policy decisions, particularly with regard to resource allocation and reallocation decisions, is a fairly recent trend, dating back to the early 1990s. Effective sharing of data and information requires a commitment to openness and access at the highest levels of an institution's management. The University of Delaware's Office of Institutional Research and Planning not only enjoys that level of support and commitment from the president, provost, and executive vice president but is also encouraged to explore new sources of data and enhanced format for reporting and sharing information.

During the 1970s and early 1980s, university databases were highly centralized, and management reports were produced by the computer center and distributed to a select and highly restricted group of users. Academic and administrative managers had information for their own units but had no idea how they compared to other units within the university, to say nothing of comparator units at other institutions. In the late 1980s the newly arrived executive vice president and the assistant vice president for institutional research and planning set about opening the University's databases to extensive use by campus managers, a move that has been wholeheartedly supported by the university's provost, who arrived in the early 1990s.

Transforming a university into an institution that is comfortable sharing and using data in support of policy decisions is not an overnight phenomenon. It requires time to build trust and confidence in data where information was previously not widely accessible. This is especially true of data that are tied to issues of cost and productivity. To secure that trust and confidence, it is absolutely essential to involve the campus community in building, analyzing, and interpreting data.

In Chapter Five, Michael Middaugh described the essential elements in the University of Delaware's Budget Support Notebooks. These notebooks were the first series of data reports that gave every academic administrator on campus a university-wide perspective on teaching loads, instructional costs, and separately budgeted research and service activity. You will recall that for each academic unit on campus the notebook reports information on degrees granted; declared majors; student credit hours taught; faculty size; and expenditure data for instruction, research, and service. These data were identified at the outset as benchmarks that would be used over time to monitor departmental activity. As such, it became imperative that department chairs and their faculty, as well as college deans, play a central role in collecting and verifying the information.

The Budget Support Notebooks were intended to give each academic unit reliable information on which courses were being taught by which faculty at what overall cost to the department. Consequently, to produce reliable information, verification of individual faculty teaching loads is essential. Prior to 1985, the single most productive faculty member on campus in terms of the number of classes taught and student credit hours generated was named Staff. There was little incentive to clean up the course registration file, as it was being used for little other than general academic recordkeeping. The advent of the Budget Support Notebooks changed this. With its origin-of-instructor perspective—that is, student credit hours and other workload measures accrue to the department paying the faculty member's salary—the notebooks positively encouraged department chairs and deans to ensure that teaching file records for their units were accurate. Currently, Staff teaches but a handful out of several thousand class sections taught at the University of Delaware each semester. And these are almost invariably credit-by-examination courses and comparable offerings where the Staff designation is appropriate.

Table 6.1 is a mock-up of the course verification form that is sent to each dean and department chair at the beginning *and* end of each term, ensuring that the data are checked and verified twice. Although the sample data in Table 6.1 represent only a few faculty, the actual form asks academic managers to ensure that every instructor in every course is identified correctly. This includes instructors who meet with zero-credit labs, recitation, and discussion sections associated with the lecture portion of a course. The data are aggregated to build toward a summary table at the end of the verification form that is replicated in Table 6.2.

Table 6.2 is particularly important on two counts: it gives the manager an instant picture of the proportion of the total departmental teaching load that is done by faculty on appointment, that is, on recurring teaching contracts with the University, and deans and chairs know that these summary data are the basis for several cost and productivity ratios in the Budget Support Notebooks.

The data in these verification forms are important not only to academic managers but also to senior administrators and the provost in particular. The departmental summaries reveal instances where faculty on reduced loads are nonetheless teaching on S-contracts, that is, for overload payment. The summary also identifies undergraduate courses in violation of university policy that a minimum of ten students be enrolled. In other words, in addition to serving as a verification tool, the departmental summaries provide information that leads to more efficient and economical academic administration.

Perhaps the single area where questions most frequently arose with regard to the data in the Budget Support Notebooks was in the area of expenditures. It was not uncommon to have a chairperson argue that the department could not have spent the stipulated amount on instruction. Or the disputed area might as easily have been research or service.

To forestall any debates over data, the Office of Institutional Research and Planning developed backup financial information to the data published in the Budget Support Notebooks. Refer back to Table 5.4, which contains fictitious data for one of the university's departments. It cites instructional expenditures for fiscal year (FY) 1998 in the amount of $1,250,221 and $264 in research expenditures. Table 6.3 ties departmental expenditures to the Budget Support Notebook. Arrayed by object and function code, Table 6.3 describes in detail for the department chair precisely what the funds were spent on and for what purpose. He or she can track what proportion of faculty salary expenditures are charged to instruction and what proportion are charged to research. Of the $1,250,221 charged to instruction, he or she can easily see the breakdown between salaries and other-than-personnel costs. And you may be certain that data arrays of this sort are equally interesting to senior administrators as well. Effective stewardship of fiscal resources necessitates knowing precisely how funds are spent.

The data described in Chapter Five as components of the university's Budget Support Notebooks are now universally accepted and used on campus. The overriding operating principles established between the administration and academic units in using the data are

1. The data from a given academic or fiscal year will not be used to reward or punish an academic unit. It is acknowledged that the data from a single year may be idiosyncratic.
2. Data will be viewed over time to identify specific trends related to teaching loads and their relationship to instructional costs. Externally sponsored activity will also be examined over time as a contextual variable in examining teaching loads.
3. The variables in the Budget Support Notebooks are purely quantitative. Academic units are challenged to provide additional qualitative

Table 6.1. Departmental Workload Verification Data

Name	Rank and Course(s)	Number of Organized Sections	Tenure and Credits	Home Department and Course Type	Percent of Load	Students		Teaching Credits	S-Contract? Yes or No
						Enrolled	Credits		
Thomas Jones	Chairperson		Tenured	Sociology					
	SOC 454	1	3 hours	Lecture	100	9	27	3	No
	SOC 964	0	3–12 hours	Supervised study	100	0	3	1	No
					Total	9	30	4	
Mary Smith	Professor		Tenured	Sociology					
	SOC 201	1	3 hours	Lecture	100	246	738	3	No
	SOC 203	1	3 hours	Lecture	100	100	300	3	No
					Total	346	1,038	6	
William Davis	Professor		Tenured	Sociology					
	CSC 311	1	3 hours	Lecture	100	8	24	3	No
	Cross-listed with SOC 311								
	SOC 311	1	3 hours	Lecture	100	38	114	3	
	Cross-listed with CSC 311								
	SOC 327	1	3 hours	Lecture	100	13	39	3	No
	SOC 366	0	1–3 hours	Supervised study	100	1	1	1	No
	SOC 866	0	1–6 hours	Supervised study	100	1	3	1	No
					Total	61	181	8	

Table 6.1. (continued)

Name	Rank and Course(s)	Number of Organized Sections	Tenure and Credits	Home Department and Course Type	Percentage of Load	Students Enrolled	Students Credits	Teaching Credits	S-Contract? Yes or No
Pauline Lee	Associate Professor PSY667	1	Tenured 1 hour	Sociology Lecture	100	3	3		
	Cross-listed with SOC 667								
	SOC 341	1	3 hours	Lecture	100	37	111	3	No
	SOC 467	1	3 hours	Lecture	100	23	69	3	No
	SOC 667	1	1 hour	Lecture	100	5	5	1	No
	Cross-listed with PSY 667				Total	68	188	7	
Roger Brown	Assistant Professor SOC 467	1	Tenure track 3 hours	Sociology Lecture	100	7	21	3	No
	400 level meets with 600 level								
	SOC 667	1	3 hours	Lecture	100	1	3		No
	600 level meets with 400 level								
	SOC 213	1	3 hours	Lecture	100	77	231	3	No
	Cross-listed with WOMS 213								
	WOMS 213	1	3 hours	Lecture	100	21	63		No
	Cross-listed with SOC 213				Total	106	318	6	

**Table 6.2. Instructional Workload Summary
by Course Type and Faculty Type**

	Course Level	Students		Teaching	
		Enrolled	Credits	Credits	Sections
All faculty					
Regularly scheduled classes	Lower division	2,378	7,048	52	18
	Upper division	942	2,907	97	31
	Graduate	35	89	13	5
	Total	3,355	10,080	162	54
Supervised study	Lower division	1	3	1	
	Upper division	37	106	37	
	Graduate	19	69	19	
	Total	57	178	57	
Regular and supervised	Lower division	2,379	7,087	53	18
	Upper division	979	3,013	134	18
	Graduate	54	158	32	5
	Total	3,412	6,381	219	54
Faculty on appointment					
Regularly scheduled classes	Lower division	2,127	6,381	45	15
	Upper division	760	2,361	79	25
	Graduate	34	86	13	5
	Total	2,921	8,828	137	45
Supervised study	Lower division	1	3	1	
	Upper division	32	93	32	
	Graduate	18	63	18	
	Total	51	159	51	
Regular and supervised	Lower division	2,128	6,384	46	15
	Upper division	792	2,454	111	25
	Graduate	52	149	31	5
	Total	2,972	8,987	188	45

information that helps to explain trend information on teaching loads and cost-productivity data.

So comfortable are academic managers with the budget support data that there are now ongoing conversations to identify additional nonfiscal variables that transcend departments and that may serve as contextual information in looking at teaching loads and instructional costs. These include nonexternally sponsored scholarship, particularly in the arts and humanities; academic advising activity; dissertation and thesis supervision; and university service.

Extending the Data

For data to be most effective for use by senior administration, the information has to be provided within a comparative context. How productive or cost effective is an academic or administrative unit? The question can best be answered by further asking, compared with what? The university's Budget

Table 6.3. Departmental Expenditures by Object and Function

Expenditures	Instruction (01–08) ($)	Departmental Research (09) ($)	Organized Activity Educational Departments (10) ($)	Research (21–39) ($)	Public Service (41–43) ($)	Academic Support (51–56) ($)
Salaries						
Professionals	137,383	57	0	23,818	0	0
Faculty						
Full-time (including department chair)	827,565	0	0	0	0	0
Part-time (including overload)	20,047	948	0	50,858	0	0
Graduate students	125,578	366	0	55,573	0	0
Postdoctoral fellows	0	0	0	0	0	0
Tuition and scholarship	0	3,030	0	0	0	0
Salaried and hourly staff	31,689	11,730	0	0	0	0
Fringe benefits	3,271	5,404	0	18,375	0	0
Subtotal	1,145,533	21,535	0	148,624	0	0
Support						
Miscellaneous wages	2,827	360	0	8,837	0	0
Travel	18,691	2,573	0	7,603	0	0
Supplies and expenses	57,877	27,311	0	20,076	0	0
Occupancy and maintenance	3,623	0	0	0	0	0
Equipment	0	0	0	0	0	0
Other expenses	19,299	27,186	0	690	0	0
Credits and transfers	-512	0	0	0	0	0
Subtotal	101,805	57,430	0	37,206	0	0
Indirect costs	2,883	0	0	78,193	0	0
Total expenditures	1,250,221	78,965	0	264,023	0	0

Support Notebooks provide data that enable us to compare one department to another within our own institution. The next logical step is to compare departments with like units at other institutions.

The discussion in Chapter Five on the uses of comparative data examines the Delaware Study of Instructional Costs and Productivity, which collects detailed data on teaching loads, costs, and productivity by academic discipline from colleges and universities across the nation. The University of Delaware was so committed to this project that the executive vice president funded the data collection until adequate external funding sources could be identified. Now a mature data consortium, the Delaware Study continues to be part of the university's public service mission.

The Office of the Provost finds it particularly useful to marry data from the Budget Support Notebooks with data from the Delaware Study to create departmental profiles that serve as tools of inquiry for more fully understanding the position of our academic units relative to each other and to comparable units outside of the University. Figure 5.2 illustrates the type of trend information generated by the Office of Institutional Research and Planning and that is provided to the provost for use in discussions with deans and chairs. The graphics in Figure 5.2, which is taken directly from the provost's notebook, quickly provide the following information:

- The departmental teaching load for tenured and tenure-track faculty at the University of Delaware, as measured in student credit hours taught, is heavier than the national benchmark for research universities.
- The direct cost per student credit hour taught at the University of Delaware is higher than the national benchmark.
- The ratio of full time–equivalent (FTE) students taught to FTE faculty (all categories) is somewhat higher than the national benchmark.
- Sponsored activity per tenured and tenure-track faculty at the university is more than twice the national benchmark.
- The number of organized class sections taught by tenured and tenure-track faculty at the university mirrors the national benchmark.
- Virtually all of the teaching is done by tenured and tenure-track faculty.

This quick snapshot tells the provost that the higher direct cost of instruction at the university should be viewed within the context of a tenured and tenure-track faculty that teaches heavier loads and brings in more research dollars than the national benchmarks. These sorts of comparative data are extremely valuable to senior administrators making resource allocation and reallocation decisions. And the data have even greater power when they are cast in trend lines over time.

However, as we noted earlier, the University of Delaware treats these benchmarks as exactly what they are—quantitative measures that do not address the qualitative dimension of an academic program or department.

We have therefore created a process of academic program review wherein we have challenged dean, department chairs, and program coordinators to do the following:

1. Identify those variables that address the qualitative aspects of the academic program. The variables can be either quantitative or qualitative but must be both measurable and amenable to benchmarking.
2. Identify six to ten institutions with academic departments or programs that are currently comparable to that at the University of Delaware.
3. Identify six to ten institutions with academic departments or programs to which that at the University of Delaware aspires to be compared.

The Office of the Provost, working with the Office of Institutional Research and Planning, is currently weaving this data collection challenge into the academic program review process. The intent is to assist academic departments and programs to define where they currently are—both quantitatively and qualitatively—with regard to resources, funding, teaching loads, research and scholarship outcomes, and other measures of their choosing. The process will provide a road map with regard to what the university's senior administration and the departments themselves must do to make the transition from their current comparator pool to the aspiration group of departments.

The academic program review procedures have generally been positively received. And why not? Deans and chairs have been told to identify the appropriate variables to define quality and to select their own benchmarking pool. Of course, we've received the standard responses, "You can't measure what we do" and "We're so unique that we don't compare to anyone." Quite candidly, we have told our departments that such positions are simply untenable. We can and must measure what we do—both in terms of how much and how well. When a parent, legislator, or university trustee asks, "How do you *know* that you're doing a good job?" the response must, in our view, go beyond the anecdotal. It must be systematic and thorough. It must address the teaching process and the outcomes of instruction in terms of job placement of graduates and employer satisfaction with their skills. For those who pursue graduate education, where they choose to study and what they do beyond graduate school are important measures. In terms of faculty scholarship, research, and service, it is not enough to simply talk in terms of the volume of external dollars received. The discussion must also include the quality of that activity, as measured by the National Research Council and other objective sources, as well as the economic and social impact of those activities on the community, the state, and the region.

These sorts of measures are perhaps more difficult to get than purely quantitative data. But they are essential components to making effective and appropriate internal policy decisions and describing the higher education enterprise to those outside of the academy.

Administrative Data Considerations

As is the case with academic policy decisions, administrative policy at the University of Delaware looks for the best available quantitative and qualitative data to inform the decision-making process. Many of the comparative databases cited in Chapter Five are used regularly and extensively at the university. These include, but are not limited to, the following:

- Faculty and staff compensation data from the College and University Personnel Association (CUPA) and the American Association of University Professors (AAUP)
- Financial ratio data from KPMG Peat Marwick
- Facilities space and staffing benchmarks from the Association of Physical Plant Administrators

In addition to comparative data, the university's Office of Institutional Research and Planning and the Budget Office generate a number of reports that are essential to monitoring fiscal resources and utilizing them most effectively. Although the AAUP and CUPA data provide valuable information on the university's competitive position in the marketplace with regard to compensation matters, additional analyses are essential to addressing issues such as salary equity, compression, and inversion. Appropriate analytical tools, such as multiple-regression models, have been created for examining equity issues not only for faculty but for professional and classified staff as well.

Similarly, the rapidly changing technological environment in which we operate can quickly transform the nature and scope of employee duties and responsibilities. The employee classification systems at any institution must be regularly examined to ensure that position descriptions are up-to-date and that current classification levels match what employees actually do. Where the classification system has become out of sync, adjustments must be identified along with the financial implications of those adjustments. At the University of Delaware, those analyses fall to the Office of Institutional Research and Planning.

In making administrative policy decisions, cost data may not be readily accessible. This is particularly true in the area of technology. Although it intuitively makes sense that appropriate use of computer and other forms of technology can result in cost savings through more effective and efficient operating procedures and use of personnel, costing out such a hypothesis can be difficult.

Consider the University of Delaware's Student Services Building. In the late 1980s, the university determined that it was time to replace the existing student records system. Shortly thereafter, the decision was made by the president and executive vice president that this was an opportune time to transform student services at the university into a totally customer-oriented operation. In a parallel effort, the university was engaged in totally modernizing the technological infrastructure of the entire campus. All facilities, including residence halls, have been networked for access to the Internet. And a Student Services Center was created that brought together representatives from offices (admissions, financial aid, registration, billing and collection, dining services, parking, and so on) that heretofore had reported to several different vice presidents and whose contact with each other had been minimal. The leadership of these units worked together to understand what was needed to provide outstanding student service. They recommended changes to policies and procedures, implemented new systems, and retrained staff.

As a result, a student who previously would have had to visit multiple offices to register for courses, pay bills, sign up for a meal plan, and the like can now visit the Student Services Building where virtually all of his or her needs are met by one person or through self-sufficient use of computer kiosks. Today, students can access transcripts, drop or add courses, inquire about bills, and more, all from their dormitory room or through Internet access to the university from off-campus sites.

Costing the student services initiative is complex. Certainly, one would need to look at expenditures related to networking the campus and constructing the Student Services Building. The cost of retraining personnel associated with the Student Services Building would also need to be factored into the equation. Over time, savings resulting from personnel streamlining associated with the enhanced technology would need to be calculated, as would reduction in paper flow. At the same time, one must consider student satisfaction with services. Since 1990, each administration of the American College Testing Program's *Student Opinion Survey* has revealed that not only have student satisfaction scores for every service related to the Student Services Building reached a new high but that they also have been significantly higher than the national norms for institutions comparable to the University of Delaware. It is difficult to place a price on student goodwill, the positive comments that reach into the admissions marketplace, and the improved attitude of alumni toward their alma mater.

It is clear that technology will have profound impact upon administrative operations at colleges and universities. The University of Delaware is moving toward becoming a paperless campus. For several years now, students have received their grades by e-mail and voice mail, improving the speed of delivery while saving paper and postage costs. Requisition for supplies, requests for leave, travel authorizations, and so on are all handled electronically. The university's purchase card, a credit card arrangement with a major bank, allows electronic payment of bills at the departmental level, which had historically required several layers of signature authorization. This innovation, combined with electronic capture of requisition information and faxing of purchase orders, has improved the turnaround time for purchase orders from as much as two weeks to typically two days while reducing Purchasing Department staff from fourteen to nine. There can be little doubt that institutions can effect significant savings through more effective and efficient use of personnel, technology, and time.

The university has also examined activities that are not part of the core teaching, research, and service mission to see if outsourcing is a viable and cost-effective option. Since 1991, operations including dining, bookstore, conference services, and computer maintenance have been successfully outsourced, resulting in improved services while improving financial performance.

In addition to individual examples of improving services and reducing costs, a more global measure is increases in administrative costs compared with academic spending over time. At the University of Delaware, between 1991 and 1998, administrative costs increased at an average of 2.8 percent per year, while academic program costs rose at 5.1 percent per year. During the same period the quality and timeliness of service delivery improved substantially. Clearly, process redesign accompanied by creative uses of technology permitted administrative savings that were available to be reallocated to the academic mission of the institution.

The impact of technology will also profoundly affect academic operations in ways that are difficult to envision at this time. It is clear that institutions such as the Western Governor's University, the University of Phoenix, and the Open University are offering Web-based instruction that is asynchronous, flexible, and enormously appealing to a growing population of nontraditional college students. If traditional colleges and universities choose to compete in this arena, there are very real costs. These expenditures will be associated not only with implementation of Web-based and distance education modes of instruction. Funds will also need to be budgeted for technical support, for assessment procedures to ensure that students are learning, and for a myriad of other issues that will become evident as the technology evolves.

Institutional researchers will play a central role in providing these sorts of data. The Higher Education Reauthorization Act of 1998 contains a provision for a congressionally mandated study of the impact of the costs of technology on higher education. The precise definition of the components of these costs, and the processes by which data are collected to measure them, are of concern not only to Congress. Those of us who sit in senior administrative offices will increasingly rely on data analysts who can provide us with timely and accurate information on the rapidly changing technological environment, its impact on academic and administrative operations, and associated costs.

So although existing comparative and institutional databases provide useful information on current administrative and academic operations, a host of external factors will impact the quantity and quality of cost information required for a college or university to be effective in a competitive environment. Institutional researchers and other data analysts on campus will play a central role in assisting senior management in underpinning decisions with the best available information.

DAVID E. HOLLOWELL is executive vice president at the University of Delaware.
MELVYN D. SCHIAVELLI is provost at the University of Delaware.

7

The issue of higher education costs has taken on national prominence in recent years. This chapter examines the constructs that are being employed at the national level to study the nature and scope of higher education expenditures.

To Lift the Veil: New College Cost Studies and the Quest for the Perfect Formula

Travis J. Reindl

It is fairly safe to say that college costs, prices, and the relationship between the two are among the most discussed—and debated—topics in higher education policy today. Millions of pages and untold hours of thought have been dedicated to these issues over the course of the past generation alone. The superabundance of discourse in this area is marked by two constants:

1. Colleges' and universities' costs and prices periodically rise to a prominent place on the policy agenda. Within the past fifteen years, there have been three significant federal actions related to college costs: in 1986, when Congress charged the Secretary of Education to identify the causes of price increases and procedures for minimizing them; in 1997, when Congress formed the National Commission on the Cost of Higher Education (NCCHE) to examine issues of cost and price and offer policy recommendations; and in 1998, when Congress approved an in-depth study of cost and price via the Higher Education Amendments of that year (U. S. Department of Education, 1999).

2. Analysts and observers use imagery related to darkness and obscurity to detail the difficulty of comprehensive cost measurement. In its final report, NCCHE used terms such as "veil of obscurity" and "financial opacity" in describing institutional finances, and a Washington-based think tank subtitled a 1999 primer on cost issues "Peering Inside Higher Education's Black Box" (National Commission on the Cost of Higher Education, 1998; Stringer and Cunningham, 1999). Such phraseology implies that a sort of

alchemy is at play in the pricing of colleges and universities, a financial wizardry that only a select few are privileged enough to practice.

To the cynic or the seasoned policy analyst, the latest spate of high-level attention to the college cost-price issue is nothing more than a rehashing of old issues, a phase that will generate a lot of rhetorical heat but relatively little analytical light. To others (the believers), however, the stern words of NCCHE and the lurking threat of policy intervention related to college pricing signaled that this iteration of the cost debate would be different, that there would have to be some breakthrough in coming to terms with the issues. In the two years that have passed since NCCHE concluded its work, the question of which camp is right is increasingly being asked. Two subsequent studies—the congressionally mandated College Cost Study (CCS) and the National Association of College and University Business Officers' Cost of College Project (CCP)—offer the first glimpses at an answer.

Findings of the NCCHE Report

As unsatisfying as it may be to many, the development of the CCS and CCP to date suggest that both the cynics and the believers will be vindicated at the end of the day. Why? Analyzing these instruments in the context of NCCHE's work yields the following conclusions:

- Both studies have significant methodological limitations that center around analytical scope, use of trend analysis, and accounting approach.
- External forces also limit both studies. These forces include availability of funding and participation necessary to achieve critical mass.
- NCCHE shortchanged some of the major analytical issues related to cost and price. Although commissioners devoted considerable attention to the cost-price-subsidy distinction and production cost issues, they placed relatively little emphasis on broader points such as the difference between higher education and private sector pricing models. As a result, the overall parameters of the discussion will remain limited.

In sum, analytical advances related to college costs and prices in the wake of NCCHE are likely to be incremental at best. Both CCS and CCP (provided that they are executed as planned) will facilitate only a slight lifting of the veil of obscurity cited by NCCHE. The lessons learned in the process of executing these two instruments, however, should not be overlooked or ignored.

Straight Talk: The National Commission on the Cost of Higher Education

As noted earlier, one of the constants in the ongoing discussion of college costs and prices is policymaker interest at the federal level. Washington's latest occupation with these issues can be traced to 1996, when President

Clinton made universal access to two years of postsecondary education a key part of his reelection platform. At the same time, the U.S. General Accounting Office issued a report that showed college and university tuition rising significantly faster than the rate of inflation or the price of other commodities (U.S. General Accounting Office, 1996). A media frenzy over spiraling tuition ensued, with the covers of national newsmagazines proclaiming "$1,000 a Week" and "Gouging U."

The combination of the high-profile attention and the imminent reauthorization of the Higher Education Act spurred Capitol Hill into action. In 1997, Congress enacted Public Law 105–18, which established the eleven-member NCCHE. The law charged the commission with examining a wide range of cost-related factors, including administrative spending, faculty workload and compensation, capital infrastructure and technology, financial aid, regulatory compliance, and state appropriations. Additionally, lawmakers instructed commissioners to establish a national mechanism for communicating cost and price information and to investigate and disseminate innovative methods for reducing and stabilizing tuition (U.S. Department of Education, 1999).

NCCHE's discussions focused on three major themes:

- *Defining terms.* The commission's attention in this area centered around the distinction between cost (what is spent by the institution), price (what is charged to or paid by the student), and subsidy (the difference between cost and price).
- *Identifying cost drivers.* Commissioners singled out six specific areas for analysis: people (students, faculty, and staff), financial aid, facilities, technology, regulations, and expectations. It is important to note that several of these areas have been minimally tracked or poorly defined in the past, especially the last four.
- *Demystifying the cost-price relationship.* As noted previously, the commission declared that a veil of obscurity had been drawn over colleges' and universities' finances and called on institutions to make their finances more transparent.

NCCHE's deliberations yielded five central recommendations:

1. Strengthen institutional cost control.
2. Improve market information and public accountability.
3. Deregulate higher education.
4. Rethink accreditation.
5. Enhance and simplify federal student aid.

The bulk of the analytical issues related to cost and price are subsumed in the first and second recommendations. In the area of strengthening cost control, NCCHE called on institutions, associations, and other higher education organizations to "adopt the topic of academic cost control as a research area worthy of major financial support" (National Commission on the Cost of Higher Education, 1998, p. 16). Additionally, the panel encouraged colleges and universities to conduct efficiency self-reviews, focusing on the areas enumerated previously as cost drivers.

With respect to improving market information and public accountability, NCCHE voiced concern over what it viewed as a serious paucity of timely data in key areas of analysis. To that end, commissioners made several recommendations, including the creation of a handbook detailing cost-price-subsidy nationally by institutional level and sector as well as information regarding the relationship between cost and price. Moreover, the panel called for the reconciliation of accounting approaches for public and private institutions (the Governmental Accounting Standards Board [GASB] for public institutions and the Federal Accounting Standards Board [FASB] for private institutions) to ensure greater analytical consistency (National Commission on the Cost of Higher Education, 1998).

Aftermath of the NCCHE Report

The overall tone of the NCCHE report, one of warning to colleges and universities, strongly influenced the pace and direction of subsequent analytical activity. Commissioners conveyed this sense of urgency through statements such as the following: "Members of the Commission are equally convinced that if this public concern continues, and if colleges and universities do not take steps to reduce their costs, policymakers at the federal and state levels will intervene and take up the task for them" (National Commission on the Cost of Higher Education, 1998, p. 1). Such sentiments underscored the push for immediate and demonstrable action. In other words, the threat of policy intervention led many to argue that something had to be done, whatever form it might take. The limitations of the two initiatives profiled in the following sections raise the question of whether the threat of imposed controls emphasized fast answers at the expense of complete answers.

College Cost Study. The first of these initiatives is the federal CCS, authorized in Part C, Section 131, of the Higher Education Amendments of 1998. The section of the law specific to cost measurement and analysis charges the commissioner of education statistics to conduct a national study of expenditures at higher education institutions over a three-year period. The items to be analyzed include

- Faculty-administrator salaries, benefits, and other expenses
- Academic support services
- Research
- Operations and maintenance
- Construction (including replacement cost of instructional buildings)
- Technology

The study's mandate also contains an evaluation component, which includes

- Changes over time in specified expenditure areas
- The relationship of expenditures to costs
- The relationship between institutional aid and tuition discounting and increases

The law mandated completion of the study by September 30, 2002, and armed the secretary of education with the power to levy a $25,000 fine against institutions failing to supply accurate and timely data for the study. The National Center for Education Statistics (NCES) began implementation of the law in early 1999 by issuing a request for proposals (RFP) to conduct the study. The RFP split the study into two phases: a feasibility study to identify data collection problems and explore potential models and a full-scale data collection that would include site visits to 750 institutions. The study is expected to collect approximately 250 variables (both original and derived) to fulfill the evaluation mandate. The original variables include information already collected systematically (expenditures for salaries, financial aid, operations and maintenance, and research) as well as data not yet gathered comprehensively (expenditures for construction and technology and replacement value of property). The derived variables are to include average cost of instruction per student credit hour, undergraduate production costs, subsidy levels for all undergraduates, and net price (U.S. Department of Education, 1999).

Cost of College Project. The second major initiative emanated from the higher education community, which closely followed the commission's deliberations. It is the CCP, undertaken by the National Association of College and University Business Officers (NACUBO). NACUBO launched CCP in 1999 with two primary objectives:

1. To create a new national methodology for institutions to measure cost, price, and subsidy on a per-student basis for a given year of undergraduate education
2. To assist policymakers in understanding cost and price interaction by institutional type

The underlying themes for the project have been simplicity and responsiveness. Simplicity is being stressed because of the desire for a model that can serve the needs of both internal and external stakeholders. Responsiveness is being emphasized because of the threat of policy intervention voiced by NCCHE. In fact, project leaders made the following statement in a September 1999 presentation: "Our view is that the [higher education] community MUST undertake such an effort, or the government will do it for us" (Spies and Fusco, 1999).

NACUBO pilot-tested its study instrument on a cross section of forty institutions in the summer of 1999. The pilot survey instrument contained three primary fields:

1. *Instructional and student services*—includes expenditures for undergraduates in the areas of instruction and departmental research, departmental administration, student services, libraries, allocated facilities operations and maintenance, allocated depreciation (facilities and equipment), and allocated administration.
2. *Institutional and community costs*—includes expenditures for undergraduates in the areas of culture, religious life, and recreation; museums and gardens; intercollegiate athletics (net cost); allocated facilities operations and maintenance; allocated depreciation (facilities and equipment); and allocated administration.
3. *Undergraduate financial aid costs*—includes expenditures for undergraduates in the areas of institutional aid resources, federal and state aid resources, and nongovernmental or external aid resources.

The individual components are then summed and divided by undergraduate full time–equivalent (FTE) enrollment to yield cost per student overall and in each of the three primary areas. Price per student (sticker-price undergraduate tuition) is then subtracted from total cost per student, with the difference as the amount of subsidy per student.

NACUBO has three purposes underpinning its methodological approach:

1. To calculate institutional expenditures made to educate a full-time, degree-seeking undergraduate student for an academic year
2. To show the relative position of and change in the functional components of the annual cost of educating an undergraduate student
3. To describe institutional cost in relation to price charged (National Association of College and University Business Officers, 1999).

Basic Issues Covered by NCCHE. The first analytical question that surfaces with respect to the CCP and CCS is the extent to which these studies substantively address areas of primary interest to the NCCHE. The preceding descriptions of the two studies indicate that some areas singled out by the commission are covered exhaustively, whereas others are given scant or no attention.

The ranks of issues covered by one or both of the studies include most of the major cost drivers cited by the commission. These are as follows:

• *People.* NCCHE pointed to spending related to faculty, staff, and students as a primary factor boosting costs. The CCS deals with this topic explicitly through a host of faculty-student variables, whereas the CCP treats it implicitly through expenditure items such as instruction and research, student services, and the like.

- *Technology.* The commission placed a great deal of emphasis on this driver, due in significant part to the testimony heard from institutional leaders. The CCS attempts to recap technology spending by colleges and universities in a way that has previously not been attempted in a national study, which poses significant challenges for the completion of a timely and accurate analysis. The CCP, on the other hand, does not address the subject, which is a serious limitation of this instrument.

- *Capital infrastructure.* Commissioners also expressed a great deal of interest in the role of the physical side of the university in cost increases, particularly as institutions add to their capital inventories at a staggering pace. Both studies thoroughly assess this subject, as the CCS establishes a variable for construction expenditures and replacement value of property, whereas the CCP covers areas such as operations and maintenance and allocated depreciation.

- *Financial aid and tuition discounting.* The role of financial aid and tuition discounting in driving price increases has been the subject of a long-standing debate in the higher education community, and NCCHE did not resolve this issue. Both studies also collect data in this area, with the CCP reporting per FTE undergraduate totals for institutional, state and federal, and nongovernmental aid. For its part, the CCS gathers data on institutionally funded and unfunded awards, federal and state loans, and federal and state grants.

- *Cost-price-subsidy.* Additionally, the major topic of the cost-price-subsidy distinction is addressed in both studies. In the CCP, price per FTE undergraduate is subtracted from cost per FTE undergraduate (sum of instructional and student services, institutional and community costs, and undergraduate financial aid costs) to arrive at per-FTE subsidy. In the CCS, the distinction is presented through variables such as average price per undergraduate student, undergraduate production cost, and subsidy levels.

Areas not covered by either the CCP or CCS include those that have historically been among the most difficult to measure. Among them are the following:

- *Student expectations.* The commission singled this out as a primary cost driver, but is it possible to quantify these expectations in any meaningful sense or to concretely link these expectations to institutional expenditures? It is likely that this topic was left behind by both studies because its significance in the broader cost-price picture may be outweighed by the effort required to gather information on it. As such, it is not likely to be taken up as the focus of major analysis anytime in the near future.

- *Regulatory compliance.* One of NCCHE's central recommendations was to deregulate higher education, which presupposes that colleges and universities are capable of measuring at least the relative fiscal magnitude of their regulatory burden. However, neither study took up this subject, perhaps due in part to the cost-benefit calculation cited earlier and perhaps due in part to political sensitivity to pointing an accusatory finger at the government for driving cost increases.

• *Role of accreditation.* Another primary recommendation of the commission centered around the reform of accreditation, in part because of the financial claim that the process is believed to exert on institutions. But just how much is accreditation costing U.S. higher education? Unfortunately, that question will go unanswered, as neither the CCP nor the CCS measure the fiscal impact of accreditation. As with student expectations and regulatory burden, the conventional wisdom is likely to hold that accreditation plays too small a role in the overall cost picture to warrant major analytical emphasis (National Commission on the Cost of Higher Education, 1998; U.S. Department of Education, 1999; National Association of College and University Business Officers, 1999).

Methodological Issues. Closely related to substantive coverage of NCCHE issues is a second question: How effectively do the CCP and CCS conduct their analyses in a methodological sense? The following points suggest that the quest to lift the veil of obscurity from the cost-price relationship is likely to remain an incomplete one, at least for the time being.

• *Analytical Scope.* The commission raised several concerns regarding the present state of cost-price data collection in its report, including the relative lack of attention to segments of the higher education population beyond full-time undergraduates. Indeed, the first three items of the panel's "Unfinished Agenda" are graduate education, part-time students, and nontraditional students. Unfortunately, both the CCS and the CCP are extremely limited in this respect. The CCP, for instance, restricts its data collection to FTE undergraduates, which means that issues such as relative cost by level of instruction are left untouched. The CCS, by contrast, does include variables for both full-time and part-time undergraduate students but still refers to the typical student as a full-time undergraduate. Given the well-documented shifts in the composition and attendance patterns of the nation's college population, the CCS and the CCP are likely to miss increasingly important areas with respect to cost-price impact.

• *Thoroughness and Simplicity.* Throughout its report, the commission stressed both thoroughness and simplicity, which requires an interesting balancing act for the prospective analyst. One could make the argument that the CCP and the CCS lean toward one imperative at the expense of the other. The CCP, for example, emphasizes simplicity—the pilot survey instrument contains five primary headings and occupies the front side of one page. However, areas of significant interest, such as technology spending and faculty and administrative salaries, are not specifically addressed. As a result, big-picture distinctions such as cost-price-subsidy are clearly portrayed, whereas intricate but significant issues are left behind. By contrast, the CCS runs the risk of collapsing under its own weight. With a sample size of 750 institutions and general ledger examinations required for 150 institutions in the feasibility phase alone, legitimate questions could be raised about the viability of such an initiative in the time frame allowed by Congress. Moreover, the proposed analysis entails approximately 250 variables assembled in complex statistical relationships concerned with biased estimates of parameters and variables that are not orthogonal to the dependent variable. Accordingly, would the resulting study be generally understandable to the relevant stakeholders, or would it simply perpetuate the image of higher education finance as intentionally obscure alchemy?

• *Trend Analysis.* Through its discussion of cost drivers such as technology, regulatory impact, and student expectations, NCCHE demonstrated its understanding of the potential for changing dynamics in the cost-price relationship. To that end, the ability to chart these dynamics through trend analysis is extremely important. On this count, the CCP does have the upper hand in that it is intended to facilitate trend construction through annual data collection. By contrast, the CCS is handicapped by the three-year time frame assigned to it in its authorizing statute. Such an approach raises two important questions. First, how can significant patterns and relationships be culled from a three-year analysis? Second, will the three-year window selected capture an instructive period for cost-price analysis? Some have suggested that by focusing on the second half of the 1990s, the study will miss important structural changes in revenues and expenditures, particularly for public institutions.

• *Accounting Methodologies.* It is a well-known fact that public and private higher education institutions use different accounting models for their general-purpose financial statements. Public institutions follow the protocols issued by GASB, whereas private institutions fall under the aegis of FASB. Differences between the two systems, particularly in the treatment of revenue streams and assets such as infrastructure, can complicate consistent finance reporting across sectors, as the experience of the Integrated Post Secondary Education Database Finance Survey indicates. NCES cited these consistency issues as a primary area of concern for the CCS, and they will undoubtedly plague the CCP as well (National Commission on the Cost of Higher Education, 1998; U.S. Department of Education, 1999; National Association of College and University Business Officers, 1999).

External Forces. A third analytical question relates to factors external to the survey instruments or the concepts tackled by them. What outside forces might complicate or significantly impede progress on either the CCP or CCS? Two issues warrant special consideration.

• *Available Resources.* This is especially crucial for the CCS, which relies exclusively on federal funding. Given that the original price tag for the project was originally pegged above $5 million and that the spending-cap-driven fiscal year (FY) 2000 budget provided no additional funds to NCES, it remains to be seen whether the CCS can be executed in any meaningful form. For the CCP, the challenge is to find pro bono support, external funders, internal funds, or a combination of the these to mount the type of effort needed to make it a national methodology.

• *Participation.* For the CCP, this is a significant challenge. To the extent that completing the survey instrument will require special calculations and data generations, it is difficult to tell whether the implicit threat of policy intervention cited by NACUBO will provide sufficient incentive for broad institutional participation. For this CCS, this is not an issue, as the force of law and the threat of a $25,000 fine for failure to comply is highly likely to compel institutional participation (U.S. Department of Education, 1999; National Association of College and University Business Officers, 1999).

Implications and Additional Issues: So What? Who Cares?

Provided that at least some of the studies' limitations can be overcome and the data collected, the question of just how much they will contribute to the cost measurement discourse lingers in the background. One metric for gauging impact is a straightforward two-pronged test used by veteran policy analysts:

• *The So What? test.* This refers to the utility of the findings rendered by a given study. In the cases of the CCP and CCS, the methodological and external limitations cited earlier raise significant questions regarding the ultimate usefulness of the findings. For example, how will thorough policy analysis of cost issues be hampered by studies that omit the graduate component of the higher education enterprise or cover only a three-year time frame? Perhaps more importantly, even if a satisfactory model of the cost-price relationship were identified, would it be used to inform the resource allocation processes of institutions and legislative bodies, which are political by nature? In other words, if we lift the veil of obscurity, what do we do next?

• *The Who Cares? test.* Closely related to the previous test, this one refers to the ability of a study to effectively reach target audiences. Applied here, will the CCP or CCS reach conclusions or forward models that will resonate with all of the relevant stakeholders in this iteration of the cost-price issue? It is clear that policymakers and citizens alike are seeking more and better information related to college costs and prices, but what kind of information? When analyzing and discussing college cost issues, audiences are often conflated when they should be separated. Additionally, some have posed the question of whether most Americans are worried so much about the cost and price of higher education as they are about its value.

Other Questions, Other Models

While analysts mull the question of whether the CCP and CCS can adequately answer NCCHE's primary research questions, a more basic question lurks in the background: Did NCCHE place enough emphasis on some of the fundamental cost-price issues? In the final analysis, some (such as the cost-price-subsidy distinction) received ample attention, whereas others were left behind. One of those given insufficient emphasis is that of the difference between pricing models in higher education and in the private sector. Winston (in National Commission on the Cost of Higher Education, 1998, pp. 122–123) cogently presents this distinction as follows:

Private sector: price = cost + profit
Higher education: price = cost − subsidy

Winston goes on to argue that this fundamental distinction, which runs counter to our free-enterprise intuition, must be internalized and applied, or cost analysis will be limited to production cost issues at the expense of subsidy questions. NCCHE did include this pricing-model distinction in its final report but placed far more emphasis on production cost issues in its recommendations. Indeed, three of the five (strengthen cost control, deregulate higher education, and rethink accreditation) focus on production cost, whereas only one (enhance and simplify federal student aid) addresses subsidy issues. Moreover, NCCHE's discussion of the role of state appropriations (a major component of subsidy) is cursory at best. Although subsidy analysis is perhaps the most complex and difficult issue in higher education finance, it is essential to solving the equation presented earlier (National Commission on the Cost of Higher Education, 1998).

Policymakers, analysts, and other stakeholders in the cost-price discussion should also allow for the emergence of new models to address analytical questions. One such model is the so-called cost disease theory offered by Baumol and Blackman (1995). They theorize that the price of higher education in the United States and throughout the industrialized world has risen faster than incomes and the price of other commodities because productivity in higher education has failed to keep pace with the price of its resource inputs. Moreover, they argue that higher education is not the only segment of the economy susceptible to this malady—other "handicraft activities," such as health care and personal and protective services, also suffer from costs that outstrip productivity gains. Baumol and Blackman conclude their analysis with the prediction that these handicraft activities will consume an increasing portion of our income and wealth, which will be reallocated from sectors of the economy with greater productivity gains. Theories such as these, which undoubtedly have their limitations, should be included in the cost-price discussion because of their potential to expand our base of knowledge regarding these issues.

Conclusion

The preceding discussion suggests that the analysis of cost and price is an iterative process, one in which small discoveries are made each time the issue is revisited. Such a dynamic permits both believers and cynics to point to something in support of their perspective. Each time, cynics will cite the limitations of analysis and the rehashing of old issues as cause for pessimism in this field of study. Believers, on the other hand, will argue that the execution of new studies represents success in achieving greater understanding of cost-price issues and in preventing interventionist policies.

The current iteration of the cost-price discussion neatly illustrates this dynamic. Cynics can point to the methodological and practical limitations of the CCP and CCS as failures and claim that the usual suspects have been rounded up, that the same issues will surface again in another decade or so. By contrast, believers will state that any effort that demonstrates to policymakers and the public that colleges and universities understand their costs and prices and institutional interest in containing them should be counted as an unqualified success.

The iterative nature of this quest to lift the veil of obscurity regarding the cost-price relationship, however, dictates that analysts and policymakers focus less on which camp is right or wrong and more on lessons learned. Both the CCP and CCS are likely to offer significant advances in knowledge regarding cost and price issues. For example, the attempt to collect data systematically on technology expenditures could provide a needed baseline for subsequent analyses. Moreover, increasing general awareness of conceptual distinctions such as those between cost, price, and subsidy and between higher education and private sector pricing models could represent important contributions on both the analytical and policy fronts. Perhaps the next iteration of the cost-price discussion can resolve some of the key questions raised in this iteration and move on to other questions such as the structure and role of subsidy.

At the end of the day, it is extremely important as a policy community to recognize the iterative nature of this process and to be attentive to the lessons that present themselves in each iteration. This two-pronged mandate is a daunting one, especially for a society intent on instant gratification and a polity driven by term limits, two-year election cycles, and sound bites. It is a mandate that must be met, however, because the issues at stake are more than simply dollars and cents or the ideal regression formula—they speak to our priorities regarding access to one of the nation's greatest assets. The previously mentioned veil of obscurity regarding cost and price in higher education may not be lifted in the immediate future or even in the foreseeable future, which in itself should not be seen as a failure. The real failure would come in forgetting or ignoring the insight to be gained from this particular quest to lift it.

References

Baumol, W., and Blackman, S.A.B. "How to Think About Rising College Costs." *Planning for Higher Education*, 1995, 23(4), 1–7.

National Association of College and University Business Officers. "Cost of College Project." Washington, D.C.: National Association of College and University Business Officers, 1999.

National Commission on the Cost of Higher Education. *Straight Talk About College Costs and Prices.* Phoenix, Ariz.: Oryx Press, 1998.

Spies, R., and Fusco, G. "NACUBO Cost of College Project." Paper presented at the Forum on the Future of Higher Education, Aspen, Colorado, Sept. 28, 1999.

Stringer, W., and Cunningham, A. "Cost, Price and Public Policy: Peering Inside Higher Education's Black Box." USA Group Foundation New Agenda Series, vol. 1, no. 3. Washington, D.C.: The Institute for Higher Education Policy, 1999.

U. S. Department of Education. "Solicitation, Offer, and Award (including Statement of Work): College Cost Study." (ED-99-R-0045) Washington, D.C.: U. S. Department of Education, 1999.

U. S. General Accounting Office. "Higher Education: Tuition Increasing Faster than Household Income and Public Colleges' Costs." (GAO/HEHS-96–154) Washington, D.C.: U. S. General Accounting Office, 1996.

TRAVIS J. REINDL is policy analyst at the American Association of State Colleges and Universities.

INDEX

AAUP. *See* American Association of University Professors
Academe, 58
Academic support, 25–26
Accounting costs, 9–10
Accounting methodologies, 43, 92, 97
Accounting profits, 38
Accreditation, 96, 99
Activity-based costing, 27
Administrative costs, 53–54
Administrative data, 70–71, 72, 73, 84–87
Administrative support, 25–26
AICPA. *See* American Institute of Certified Public Accountants
Allocation and reallocation decisions. *See* Resource allocation and reallocation decisions
Allocation ratios, 55, 57
American Association of State Colleges and Universities, 101
American Association of University Professors (AAUP), 58, 84
American College Testing Program, 85
American Institute of Certified Public Accountants (AICPA), 20, 21
Armstrong, K. J., 47
Aspiration group, 83
Association of Physical Plant Administrators, 71, 84
Average cost, 11

Backup data, 50, 77
Basic budget, 71, 72
Baumol, W., 99
Benchmark data, 65, 68–69, 70, 76, 82
Blackman, S.A.B., 99
Book values, 38, 39
Bowen, H. R., 14
Brinkman, P. T., 5
British Inland Revenue Department, 47
Budget support data, 64–65
Budget Support Notebooks (University of Delaware), 62, 73–74, 76–77, 80, 82
Bureaucratic accretion, 14
Buyer costs, 6

Capital costs, 9, 11, 32, 33, 36, 37–42, 43
Carleton College, 31, 38, 43

Carnegie classification, 43, 57–58, 65
Carnegie Commission on Higher Education, 9
CCP. *See* Cost of College Project
CCS. *See* College Cost Study
Clinton, W., 90–91
Collections, valuing, 42
College and University Personnel Association (CUPA), 58, 71, 84
College Cost Study (CCS), 90, 92–93, 94–100
Comparability: of academic and administrative relative growth, 73; of accounting methodologies, 43, 92, 97; of opportunity costs estimates, 40. *See also* Interinstitutional comparisons; Time and comparative data
Competitive market model, 8
Compliance reporting, 22
Congress, 86. *See also* National Commission on the Cost of Higher Education
Consortium for Financing Higher Education, 41
Constructed cost, 13
Construction price index, 39
Consumer price index (CPI), 6, 14
Consumers, students as, 6, 8
Cost: accounting, 11–12; administrative, 53–54; buyer, 6; capital, 9, 11, 32, 33, 36, 37–42, 43; categories of, 21, 22, 29; control, 91–92, 99; curves, 12; defined, 91; determining, 10, 11–13; direct, 10–11, 21–25, 82; disease theory, 99; function, 7; indirect, 10–11, 25, 53; operation and maintenance, 26, 27–28, 33, 37; opportunity, 9–10, 33, 40–42; overhead, 10, 26–27, 28–29; perspectives on, 9–11; and price, relationship of, 89–100; supplier, 5, 6, 11, 13–15
Cost of College Project (CCP), 90, 93–98, 100
Cost-per analysis, 44, 50–53, 65
Cost-price-subsidy, 91, 92, 93, 100; distinction, 90, 95, 96; at Williams College, 36, 44
Cost-productivity measures, 51–52
Course verification forms, 76–77, 78–79
CPI. *See* Consumer price index

Vanderbilt University, 58
Variable-cost components, 11

Wage differentials, 8
Web-based instruction, 86
Welfare economics, 9
Western Governor's University, 86
Williams College, 32, 34–35, 41, 42, 45n. 3, 46; and book values, 38, 39;

and cost-price-subsidy, 36, 44; versus university complexity, 31, 43, 44
Williams Project on the Economics of Higher Education, 31–32
Winston, G. C., 31
Workload data, 62, 64, 68–69, 78–80, 82

Yale University, 42

Back Issue/Subscription Order Form

Copy or detach and send to:
Jossey-Bass Publishers, 350 Sansome Street, San Francisco CA 94104-1342

Call or fax toll free!
Phone 888-378-2537 6AM-5PM PST; Fax 800-605-2665

Back issues: Please send me the following issues at $23 each
(Important: please include series initials and issue number, such as IR90)

1. IR _____

_____

_____

$ _____ Total for single issues

$ _____ Shipping charges (for single issues *only;* subscriptions are exempt
from shipping charges): Up to $30, add $5^{50} • $30^{01}–$50, add $6^{50}
$50^{01}–$75, add $8 • $75^{01}–$100, add $10 • $100^{01}–$150, add $12
Over $150, call for shipping charge

Subscriptions Please ❏ start   ❏ renew my subscription to *New Directions for
Institutional Research* for the year _____ at the following rate:

U.S.	❏ Individual $56	❏ Institutional $99
Canada:	❏ Individual $81	❏ Institutional $124
All Others:	❏ Individual $86	❏ Institutional $129

NOTE: Subscriptions are quarterly, and are for the calendar year only.
Subscriptions begin with the Spring issue of the year indicated above.

$ _____ Total single issues and subscriptions (Add appropriate sales tax
for your state for single issue orders. No sales tax for U.S. subscriptions.
Canadian residents, add GST for subscriptions and single issues.)

❏ Payment enclosed (U.S. check or money order only)

❏ VISA, MC, AmEx, Discover Card #_____ Exp. date_____

Signature _____ Day phone _____

❏ Bill me (U.S. institutional orders only. Purchase order required)

Purchase order #_____

Federal Tax ID 135593032   GST 89102-8052

Name _____

Address _____

_____

Phone_____ E-mail _____

For more information about Jossey-Bass Publishers, visit our Web site at:
www.josseybass.com   **PRIORITY CODE = ND1**

OTHER TITLES AVAILABLE IN THE
NEW DIRECTIONS FOR INSTITUTIONAL RESEARCH SERIES
J. Fredericks Volkwein, Editor-in-Chief